Maggie Beer

Maggie Beer is one of Australia's best-known cooks. In addition to co-hosting *The Cook and The Chef* and making regular appearances on *MasterChef Australia*, Maggie devotes her time to the Farmshop in the Barossa Valley where it all began, and to her export kitchen, which produces her famous pate, fruit pastes, jams, sauces and verjuice, as well as a range of super-indulgent ice creams.

Maggie is the author of seven successful cookbooks, *Maggie's Verjuice Cookbook*, *Maggie's Kitchen*, *Maggie's Harvest*, *Maggie's Table*, *Cooking with Verjuice*, *Maggie's Orchard* and *Maggie's Farm*, and co-author of the bestselling *Stephanie Alexander and Maggie Beer's Tuscan Cookbook*.

Her website is maggiebeer.com.au

LANTERN COOKERY CLASSICS

LANTERN
an imprint of
PENGUIN BOOKS

BEGINNING

MIDDLE

END

BASICS

Beginning

Avocado jellies

Simple as these are, these jellies are something I never tire of. There is something quite magical about the sight of perfectly ripe cubes of avocado suspended in a verjuice and French tarragon jelly.

1½ cups (375 ml) verjuice (see page 141)
2 sprigs French tarragon, plus 18 extra
    leaves for moulds
1 teaspoon caster sugar
3 × 2 g gold-strength gelatine leaves
2 large ripe avocados
squeeze of lemon juice
sea salt
extra virgin olive oil and chervil sprigs
    or micro herbs (optional), to serve

1 Place verjuice, tarragon sprigs and sugar in a small stainless-steel saucepan over low–medium heat, then bring just to a simmer, being careful not to let it boil or the verjuice will become cloudy. Remove from heat and set aside to infuse for 10 minutes.

2 Soak gelatine leaves in a small bowl of cold water for 5 minutes until softened. Remove gelatine and squeeze out excess liquid. Add to warm verjuice, then stir until gelatine has dissolved. Remove tarragon and discard. Set aside to cool to room temperature.

3 Cut avocados into 5 mm dice and squeeze with a little lemon juice to stop them discolouring.

4 Have ready six 125 ml moulds. Place 3 tarragon leaves in the base of each mould and distribute avocado evenly among moulds. Carefully divide verjuice mixture among moulds. Cover each mould with plastic film, pressing it lightly down onto the surface.

5 Refrigerate jellies for 4 hours or until set.

6 To turn jellies out of moulds, dip base of each mould in a bowl of hot water for 30 seconds, then invert each jelly onto a serving plate. Season with salt, drizzle with olive oil and scatter with chervil sprigs or micro herbs, if using, before serving.

Broccoli with almonds and lemon butter

I must admit to preferring the broccoli stalks over the heads, but when tossed in a pan with nut-brown butter, almonds and lemon juice, I'll gladly eat every bit. This is delicious served alongside char-grilled or barbecued lamb.

50 g flaked almonds
1 head broccoli, cut into florets
sea salt
100 g unsalted butter, chopped
extra virgin olive oil, for cooking
juice of 1 lemon
sea salt and freshly ground black pepper

1 Preheat a fan-forced oven to 180°C (200°C). Place flaked almonds on a baking tray and roast for 5 minutes or until golden, then set aside to cool.

2 Blanch broccoli in a saucepan of boiling salted water.

3 Meanwhile, melt butter with a splash of olive oil in a frying pan over medium–high heat. Add flaked almonds and toss, then drain broccoli and immediately add to pan. Deglaze pan with lemon juice, then transfer to a serving dish and serve immediately, seasoned with salt and pepper.

Braised waxy potatoes

The secret to the success of this dish is the flavour of the potatoes you use. For me, Nicolas are the first variety I seek out, perhaps because they are grown here in the Barossa. From late January, when Nicolas are in season, I'm first in the queue at the potato stall at our local Saturday markets. This is such a delicious dish that it deserves to be served as the star of a meal in its own right. It only needs something really simple alongside – a perfectly grilled lamb chop for instance, or the Beef in the Italian Style on page 72.

500 g waxy potatoes (such as Nicolas, Dutch creams or Kipflers), halved or quartered, depending on size
1½ cups (375 ml) Golden Chicken Stock (see page 132)
2 fresh bay leaves
40 g unsalted butter, chopped
extra virgin olive oil, for cooking
sea salt
1 tablespoon finely chopped thyme
¼ cup (3 tablespoons) roughly chopped flat-leaf parsley
squeeze of lemon juice
freshly ground black pepper

1 Preheat a fan-forced oven to 180°C (200°C).

2 Place potato in a small deep baking dish so it fits snugly; the potato needs to be submerged in stock. Add stock, bay leaves, butter, a good splash of olive oil and a pinch or two of salt. Bake for 60–90 minutes until tender (the exact time will depend on the variety and size of potatoes used), basting with cooking liquid every now and again.

3 Sprinkle with thyme, parsley and lemon juice, then season to taste and serve.

Salad of beetroot, blood orange and pumpkin

I find a million ways to bring roast pumpkin into my diet – it's finding a good pumpkin that's the hard part. So when I see a great pumpkin (freshly cut to show depth of colour and ripeness), I take it home to cook with whatever else is in season. Here I've also used beetroot, another of my favourites, and blood oranges too – their amazing colour and sweet-sour notes complement any dish they are added to.

1 bunch baby beetroot, leaves trimmed leaving
     2 cm stalks attached (this prevents them
     from 'bleeding' into the water)
sea salt
2 tablespoons red-wine vinegar
extra virgin olive oil, for drizzling
470 g Kent or Queensland blue pumpkin, seeded
     and cut into 3 × 3.5 cm-thick wedges
¼ cup (3 tablespoons) sage leaves
60 g unsalted butter, chopped
2 blood oranges, thinly sliced widthways
1 tablespoon chopped chives
1 bunch watercress, sprigs picked
1 head witlof (chicory), outer leaves discarded
     and inner leaves separated

VINAIGRETTE
1 tablespoon honey
¼ cup (60 ml) extra virgin olive oil
2 tablespoons red-wine vinegar
sea salt and freshly ground black pepper

1 Place beetroot in a saucepan of salted water with 1 tablespoon of the vinegar added and bring to the boil. Reduce heat to low and cook for 50 minutes or until tender. The beetroot are ready when a skewer inserts easily into the largest one. Drain beetroot and place in a bowl of cold water, then leave to cool slightly before slipping skins off by hand. Cut into quarters, drizzle with remaining vinegar and a splash of olive oil, then sprinkle with salt and set aside.

2 Preheat a fan-forced oven to 200°C (220°C).

3 Meanwhile, cut pumpkin wedges in half widthways, then place on a baking tray, drizzle with olive oil, sprinkle with salt and roast for 20 minutes or until cooked and coloured but still firm. Leave to cool, then peel.

4 Place sage leaves on a baking tray and dot with small pieces of butter. Bake for 8 minutes or until butter starts to sizzle and sage leaves are crisp; take care as they burn easily.

5 Mix beetroot, pumpkin, blood orange, chives, watercress and witlof in a serving bowl.

6 For the vinaigrette, combine all ingredients in a small bowl and season to taste. Add enough dressing to salad to just coat, then toss to combine. Scatter with crisp sage leaves, divide among plates and serve.

Carrots in verjuice with goat's cheese and pine nuts

This dish is a great accompaniment to any meal. The addition of currants, pine nuts and goat's cheese transforms it into a wonderful luncheon dish in its own right.

¼ cup (35 g) dried currants
⅓ cup (80 ml) verjuice (see page 141)
1 bunch baby (dutch) carrots, green tops
    trimmed (leave about 2 cm), scrubbed
sea salt
¼ cup (40 g) pine nuts
100 g unsalted butter, chopped
½ cup (100 g) marinated chevre
    or fresh goat's curd
extra virgin olive oil, for drizzling
¼ cup (3 tablespoons) chopped
    flat-leaf parsley

1 Place currants and verjuice in a small bowl and leave to plump.

2 Cook carrots in a saucepan of boiling salted water for 5 minutes or until almost cooked through. To check, remove a carrot, then rub with a clean Chux; if cooked, the skin will easily peel off. Leave carrots to cool a little, then use a Chux to rub skins off while still warm. Set aside to cool, then halve lengthways.

3 Drain currants, reserving verjuice. Toast pine nuts in a frying pan over low heat until golden. Transfer to a bowl, then add butter to pan and melt over medium heat until bubbling but not nut-brown. Add carrot to pan and increase heat to high, then cook for 2–3 minutes or until butter turns nut-brown. Add reserved verjuice and cook until reduced and syrupy. Add currants and pine nuts then transfer to a serving dish. Top with chevre or spoon over goat's curd and drizzle with olive oil. Scatter over the parsley and serve at once.

Olive tart

Fresh local garlic is the real hero of this dish. From November through to February or March in the Barossa, the Marschall boys sell their highly sought-after heads of fresh pink-hued garlic at our produce markets. After using such amazing garlic, I am unable to bring myself to use the bleached imported stuff that is so inferior. If local garlic isn't available I stop to think whether I want to add garlic to a dish at all. Seek out local garlic at farmers' markets during summer. It keeps for months if stored in a dry, dark, airy spot.

**350 g bought butter puff pastry, thawed
(I use Carême, made here in the Barossa)
2 whole heads garlic, cloves separated
extra virgin olive oil, for drizzling
1 egg, lightly beaten
1 cup (150 g) black olives, pitted
zest of 1 orange, removed in thin strips with
a vegetable peeler, leaving the bitter pith
2 tablespoons oregano leaves, roughly chopped,
plus extra leaves to serve
1 tablespoon rosemary leaves (optional)
80 g marinated Persian goat's feta**

1 Roll out pastry until 2.5 mm thick. Cut a 3 cm wide strip from each side of the pastry sheet. Place the trimmed pastry sheet on a baking tray lined with baking paper, then position the 4 strips on edges of pastry sheet to create a border. Prick base of pastry thoroughly with a fork. Refrigerate for several hours or pop in the freezer for 15 minutes.

2 Blanch garlic cloves in a saucepan of boiling water for 5 minutes. Drain, leave until cool enough to handle, then peel; the skins will easily slip off. Place garlic in the smallest frying pan you have, drizzle generously with olive oil, cover and simmer over low heat for 10–15 minutes or until golden, then leave to cool.

3 Preheat fan-forced oven to 220°C (240°C).

4 Brush pastry border with egg. Bake pastry for 20 minutes, then dot with peeled garlic. Toss olives with orange zest, oregano, rosemary leaves, if using, and a drizzle of olive oil, then scatter evenly over pastry base. Place spoonfuls of goat's feta over filling. Bake for 10 minutes, then reduce oven temperature to 200°C fan-forced (220°C) and bake for another 10 minutes or until pastry is deep golden.

5 Add a final drizzle of olive oil, then scatter with extra oregano leaves and serve.

Ricotta and basil frittata

The combination of good-quality ricotta, our own free-range eggs and basil from the garden means I am more likely to make this frittata than an omelette, particularly as it feeds everyone at once!

375 g whole-milk ricotta
8 large eggs
½ cup (40 g) freshly grated Parmigiano Reggiano
12 basil leaves
sea salt and freshly ground black pepper
freshly grated nutmeg
1 tablespoon extra virgin olive oil
sliced tomatoes and basil sprigs (optional),
   to serve

1 If the ricotta you bought doesn't come in a perforated mould through which the whey can drain, tip it into a clean square of muslin or Chux. Tie up corners and hang ricotta over a bowl to drain for 10 minutes.

2 Break eggs into a bowl and beat lightly with a fork, then add drained ricotta and Parmigiano. Tear basil and add to bowl. Season with salt, pepper and nutmeg and mix well with a wooden spoon.

3 Heat olive oil in a frying pan – you should only have a film over the base – until it sizzles. Tip egg mixture into pan and turn heat down a little. Keep piercing bottom of mixture with a fork as the egg begins to set to allow the liquid on top to seep down. Cook until almost set.

4 Remove pan from heat, then, holding a dinner plate over the pan, flip frittata onto the plate. Slide frittata back into pan with undercooked side to the heat and cook for just a moment. Repeat the trick with the dinner plate and turn the frittata out to serve. Serve with sliced tomato and basil sprigs, if desired, and a final grinding of pepper.

Eggplant, roasted tomato and 'rag' pasta with buffalo mozzarella

SERVES 4 AS AN ENTRÉE

Summer is the perfect time to marry eggplant with slow-roasted tomatoes. Here I've also added buffalo mozzarella as a visit to Victoria's Shaw River Buffalo Cheese has made me a lifelong advocate of this special cheese. Homemade rag pasta transforms the simple flavours of this dish into something quite spectacular.

8 roma (plum) tomatoes, halved lengthways
¼ cup (3 tablespoons) roughly chopped oregano
extra virgin olive oil, for frying and drizzling
sea salt and freshly ground black pepper
1 quantity Fresh Pasta (see page 137)
2 eggplants (aubergines), about 12 cm × 8 cm,
    peeled and cut widthways into 2 cm wide slices
1 clove garlic, finely chopped
¼ cup (3 tablespoons) basil leaves,
    plus extra to serve
200 g buffalo mozzarella or chevre, at room
    temperature and torn

1 Preheat fan-forced oven to 150°C (170°C).

2 Place tomato, cut-side up, on a baking tray, then scatter with 1 tablespoon of the oregano, drizzle with olive oil and season with salt and pepper. Roast for 1–4 hours, depending on the level of moisture of the tomatoes.

3 Cut pasta sheets into irregular pieces or 'rags', then cover with a tea towel and set aside.

4 Meanwhile, if desired, soak eggplant in salted water (I add 1 tablespoon salt to every 600 ml water) for 30 minutes; this helps prevent it from absorbing excessive oil during cooking. Dry eggplant well. Working in batches, fry eggplant in a splash of olive oil in a hot frying pan until cooked, then drain on paper towel. Place warm eggplant, garlic, basil and remaining oregano in a bowl and toss.

5 Cook the 'rags' in a large saucepan of generously salted water for about 3 minutes, then drain and return to pan (reserve a little cooking water to bind the sauce, if desired) and drizzle with olive oil. Place pasta, eggplant mixture, tomato and half of the mozzarella in a large bowl, season to taste and gently combine.

6 Divide pasta among 4 plates, top with remaining mozzarella, then serve with a final drizzle of olive oil and perhaps a few extra basil leaves.

Grape schiacciata

I thought I could make grape schiacciata until a dinner at our friends the Parronchis in Tuscany, where we celebrated the olive crush of mutual friends, Janet and Stefano. I cooked guinea fowl my way, and Stefano brought a huge slab of schiacciata. It was so good, I wrote down all the advice I could glean from him.

20 g fresh or 2 teaspoons dried yeast
¾ cup (180 ml) warm water
1 teaspoon caster sugar, plus extra
    for sprinkling
150 ml extra virgin olive oil, plus extra
    for greasing
2 tablespoons finely chopped rosemary
2⅔ cups (400 g) unbleached strong flour,
    plus extra for dusting
pinch of salt
1 kg ripe black grapes, washed well,
    stems removed
small sprigs rosemary, for scattering

1 Combine yeast, warm water and caster sugar in a small bowl and set aside for 5–10 minutes until frothy. Warm olive oil in a saucepan and gently cook the rosemary for 5 minutes, then set aside to cool.

2 Place flour and salt in a bowl, then make a well and add the yeast mixture and half the rosemary-infused oil. Add 400 g of the grapes and mix vigorously, then turn the dough out onto a well-floured bench. Knead grapes into dough for 5 minutes – the dough will be very soft and sticky (don't use an electric mixer with a dough hook as it will smash the grapes).

3 Return dough to cleaned and lightly oiled bowl and brush with a little rosemary oil. Cover bowl with plastic film and refrigerate dough overnight or allow it to rise slowly in a warm place for 1½–2 hours until doubled in volume.

4 If you have let your dough rise in the refrigerator, allow it to come to room temperature (this will take about 1½ hours). Turn out dough and divide into 2 portions (there's no need to knock back). Generously brush 2 ovenproof frying pans or 24 cm springform cake tins with rosemary oil and, using your hands, flatten a piece of dough out over base of each pan. Push remaining grapes into surface of dough.

5 Generously brush dough with remaining rosemary oil, then sprinkle over rosemary sprigs and 1 tablespoon caster sugar. Leave to rise in a draught-free spot for about 30 minutes. Meanwhile, preheat fan-forced oven to 220°C (240°C).

6 Bake the schiacciate for 20 minutes on a baking tray as the juice from the grapes will bubble up and may overflow. Reduce oven temperature to 180°C (200°C) and bake for a further 10 minutes. Slide out onto a wire rack and serve warm or at room temperature.

Baked olives

This dish is a variation on a favourite theme of mine, that of matching olives with citrus zest. Sometimes I also add nuts such as walnuts.

2 cups (160 g) pickled olives
2 cloves garlic, finely chopped
zest of 1 orange, removed in thin strips with
**   a vegetable peeler, leaving the bitter pith**
4 fresh bay leaves
⅓ cup (80 ml) extra virgin olive oil
2 tablespoons verjuice (see page 141)
**   or lemon juice**
picked rosemary leaves, to serve

1 Preheat fan-forced oven to 180°C (200°C). Toss together olives, garlic, orange zest, bay leaves, olive oil and verjuice or lemon juice. Place in a baking dish and bake for 5–10 minutes. Leave to cool just a little before serving. If all the moisture is absorbed, add extra olive oil and verjuice or lemon juice along with the rosemary, then serve with drinks.

Green bean salad with seared tuna, pullet eggs and wild olives

I hesitate to call this a Nicoise salad, but that is, of course, its base. The first beans of late spring always make me want to serve this – while keeping their colour is vital, so is making sure they are cooked. In contrast, the tuna should be quite rare in the centre.

400 g green beans, topped, tailed
   and halved, if very long
sea salt
4 pullet eggs
1 small handful basil leaves, shredded
250 g cherry tomatoes, halved
4 × 150 g thick tuna steaks
½ cup (125 ml) extra virgin olive oil
1 tablespoon red-wine vinegar
freshly ground black pepper
handful small wild olives

1 Blanch beans in a pan of boiling salted water until tender, then drain well. Set aside. Cook eggs in a pan of simmering salted water for 4 minutes, then drop into cold water to inhibit cooking (they should be soft-boiled).

2 Keep a little basil aside, then toss beans with tomato and remaining basil and divide among 4 plates.

3 Drizzle tuna steaks with 1 tablespoon of the olive oil and heat a non-stick frying pan until very hot. Sear tuna for 2 minutes on first side, then season and turn and cook for 1 minute only. The steaks will be rare in the centre. Leave to rest for 5 minutes, then cut into chunks and toss with remaining basil.

4 Whisk remaining olive oil with vinegar, then season with salt and pepper. Gently toss tuna chunks with bean salad, then cut eggs in half and add to the top and drizzle over vinaigrette. Add olives, then serve with salt and pepper on the table.

There is a huge difference between fresh and frozen scallops. Frozen scallops release moisture when they cook, so they're more likely to poach than fry. Sadly, you sometimes see frozen scallops sold as fresh, so try to buy from a fishmonger who can vouch for the freshness of the catch.

12 scallops on the half-shell, roe intact
finely grated zest of 1 lime
1 tablespoon extra virgin olive oil,
**   plus extra for drizzling**
sea salt and freshly ground black pepper
80 g unsalted butter
⅓ cup (80 ml) verjuice (see page 141)
chervil leaves, to serve

PRESERVED LEMON AND CAPER BUTTER
1 quarter preserved lemon (see page 141),
**   flesh removed and rind rinsed**
100 g unsalted butter, softened and chopped
1 teaspoon salted capers, rinsed
1 tablespoon verjuice (see page 141)
1 tablespoon chervil leaves

1 For the preserved lemon and caper butter, process all ingredients in a food processor until well combined. Transfer to a sheet of plastic film and roll into a 3 cm-thick log, then wrap in baking paper and chill in the refrigerator for at least 30 minutes to firm up or until ready to use.

2 Meanwhile, to clean scallops, pull meat away from shell, then cut out and discard dark intestinal tract, keeping roe intact. Wash and dry shells, then spread in a single layer on a baking tray. Toss scallops with lime zest and olive oil in a bowl, then season with salt and pepper.

3 Preheat fan-forced oven to 180°C (200°C).

4 Melt half of butter in a frying pan over high heat until sizzling, then add a splash of extra olive oil to stop butter burning. Add 6 scallops and cook on one side for 30 seconds or until golden around edges, then turn and cook for a further 30 seconds. Remove from pan and place each scallop on a scallop shell. Add half of verjuice and cook, stirring, for 1 minute or until evaporated slightly, then pour over scallops. Wipe out pan with paper towel and quickly repeat process with remaining butter, scallops, shells and verjuice.

5 Top each scallop with a generous slice of preserved lemon and caper butter and place in oven for 1 minute or just until butter begins to melt. Top each scallop with a chervil leaf and serve at once.

Grilled vegetables with verjuice and extra virgin olive oil

We tend to eat outside most weeknights in summer and autumn. No matter how rushed the day has been, life is definitely too short not to take the time to enjoy good food every day and this dish is a perfect example. Cook all the vegetables on the barbecue grill plate following the order I've given here so they are ready at the same time.

2 small red onions, halved crossways
2 bulbs baby fennel, trimmed, halved lengthways
    or 1 large bulb, cut lengthways into 1.5 cm
    thick slices, fronds reserved to garnish
2 Japanese eggplants (aubergines), sliced
    lengthways, flesh scored
2 small or 1 large red capsicum (pepper), halved
    lengthways (if large, cut into quarters),
    white membrane and seeds removed
2 small zucchini (courgettes), halved lengthways
⅔ cup (160 ml) extra virgin olive oil
sea salt

POST-COOKING MARINADE
⅔ cup (160 ml) extra virgin olive oil
⅔ cup (160 ml) verjuice (see page 141)
1 lemon (preferably Meyer), cut in half
    and thinly sliced
small handful roughly chopped
    flat-leaf parsley

1 Preheat a barbecue grill plate to high.

2 Place onion, fennel, eggplant, capsicum and zucchini in a large roasting pan or mixing bowl, then add olive oil and toss to coat well. Season with salt.

3 Place onion, cut-side down, on the barbecue and grill for 15–20 minutes. After 5 minutes, add fennel and cook for 10–15 minutes, then add eggplant and cook for 10–12 minutes. Add capsicum and cook for 8 minutes or until the skin blackens and blisters, then remove from barbecue and peel off skin. Finally, add zucchini and cook for 6–8 minutes: turn over all vegetables except onion halfway through cooking.

4 Meanwhile, for the post-cooking marinade, whisk olive oil and verjuice together in a large shallow dish, then add lemon and parsley and set aside.

5 Remove vegetables from the grill plate as they are ready and place in post-cooking marinade. Gently toss to coat.

6 Transfer warm vegetables to a platter, drizzle with marinade and garnish with lemon, parsley and reserved fennel fronds. Serve.

Fennel with goat's curd

One of my favourite ways to cook fennel is to gently poach it in extra virgin olive oil and verjuice at a simmer, as I have done here.

⅓ cup (80 ml) extra virgin olive oil
1 large, plump bulb fennel, trimmed and
    cut into quarters, fronds reserved
4 fresh bay leaves
1 Meyer lemon (optional), cut into thin wedges
sea salt and freshly ground black pepper
¼ cup (60 ml) verjuice (see page 141)
    or fruity white wine
100 g goat's curd
baby purple basil or chopped flat-leaf parsley,
    to serve

1 Heat a little of the olive oil in a heavy-based frying pan over low heat, then gently seal fennel quarters on each side. Add fennel fronds, bay leaves and lemon, if using, then season with salt and pepper.

2 Add verjuice or white wine and remaining olive oil, then cover and simmer for 20 minutes or until cooked through. Remove the lid, then increase heat to high and cook for another 5 minutes or until fennel is coloured and pan juices are reduced to a syrup.

3 Remove fennel, season to taste and serve as a warm salad, topped with spoonfuls of goat's curd and baby purple basil or chopped parsley.

I like to serve asparagus with hollandaise. When I do, I begin to make the hollandaise just as I put the water for cooking the asparagus on to boil.

1 tablespoon sea salt
ice cubes
2 bunches fat asparagus, woody ends discarded
extra virgin olive oil, for brushing
freshly ground black pepper

VERJUICE HOLLANDAISE

1½ cups (375 ml) verjuice (see page 141)
1 fresh bay leaf
6 black peppercorns
250 g unsalted butter, chopped
4 egg yolks
sea salt and freshly ground white pepper

1 For the hollandaise, combine verjuice, bay leaf and peppercorns in a stainless-steel saucepan, then bring to the boil and reduce over high heat to 2 tablespoons of liquid. Strain and set aside. Gently melt butter in a small saucepan over very low heat, then leave to cool a little. Skim off any white scum floating on top, then carefully pour the clear liquid that remains into another small saucepan, leaving behind as much milky-white sediment as possible. Discard sediment and keep melted butter warm.

2 Bring a deep saucepan of water to the boil and add the salt. Place a bowl of iced water by the stove, ready for refreshing the asparagus. Blanch asparagus by plunging it momentarily into boiling water, then quickly transfer to iced water, leave to cool, then drain.

3 Heat a chargrill plate over high heat, brush asparagus with a little olive oil, season with pepper, then chargrill.

4 Meanwhile, finish making the hollandaise. Pulse egg yolks and cooled verjuice mixture in a food processor to emulsify. Make sure butter is quite warm, then, with the motor running, add it very slowly to the egg mixture and continue processing until combined and thickened; the texture should be similar to that of mayonnaise. Season to taste.

5 Place asparagus on a plate and serve immediately with verjuice hollandaise.

Creamy fish soup

I don't often make a creamy soup these days but there's something wonderful about the flavour of fish stock, fennel and Pernod finished off with cream. Mind you, it must be a good-quality fish stock, and for me that's one made with snapper heads, as used below.

80 g unsalted butter
¼ cup (60 ml) extra virgin oil olive,
    plus extra for drizzling
1 large bulb fennel, trimmed and cut
    into 5 mm thick slices
2 large waxy potatoes (such as Dutch creams),
    peeled and cut into 3 cm pieces
sea salt
¼ cup (60 ml) verjuice (see page 141)
¼ cup (60 ml) Pernod
3½ cups (875 ml) Fish Stock (see page 133)
¾ cup (180 ml) thickened cream
freshly ground white pepper
1 × 120 g salmon fillet, skin removed
    and pin-boned
4 raw prawns, peeled and cleaned,
    with tails intact
4 scallops, trimmed and cleaned
chervil leaves (optional), to serve
2 lemons, cut in half and briefly grilled

1 Melt 40 g butter with 2 tablespoons olive oil in a large heavy-based saucepan over medium heat. Add fennel and cook for 4 minutes, stirring so it doesn't brown. Add potato and cook for a further 2 minutes, then add 2 good pinches of salt. Add verjuice and Pernod, increase heat to high and cook for 3–4 minutes, stirring, until liquid has reduced by about half.

2 Pour in fish stock and bring to the boil, then reduce heat to low–medium and simmer for 30–40 minutes or until fennel and potato are very tender. Stir through cream, then, using a stick blender, puree soup until smooth. Taste and adjust the seasoning with salt and white pepper if needed, then cover and keep warm.

3 Heat remaining butter and olive oil in a non-stick frying pan over medium–high heat until butter has melted. Reduce heat to medium, then cook salmon for 2–3 minutes on each side or until cooked one-third of the way through and still pink in the centre. Transfer salmon to a paper-towel-lined plate to drain. Add prawns and scallops to pan and cook for 1½–2 minutes on each side or until just cooked through, then transfer to plate with salmon. Gently flake salmon into chunks.

4 Ladle soup into bowls, then add salmon and seafood and garnish with chervil, if using. Finish with a final drizzle of olive oil, then serve with grilled lemon halves alongside.

Vitello tonnato

Vitello tonnato is a classic Italian dish of sliced veal topped with a tuna mayonnaise. I first came across this method for cooking it in Ada Boni's *Italian Regional Cooking*, and the following recipe is my adaptation of it. Poaching the veal the day before will really enhance the flavours. Whilst I've recommended using tinned Italian tuna here, I'm always hopeful that we'll soon see good-quality Australian tuna in olive oil on our supermarket shelves.

2 × 350 g pieces nut of veal
1 onion, finely chopped
2 × 95 g tins Italian tuna in olive oil, drained
2 fresh bay leaves
1 × 45 g tin anchovies, drained
2 tablespoons salted capers, rinsed
1½ cups (375 ml) verjuice (see page 141)
    or dry white wine
1 cup (250 ml) extra virgin olive oil
2 hard-boiled egg yolks
squeeze of lemon juice
1 egg yolk
sea salt and freshly ground black pepper
1 lemon, thinly sliced
12 tiny cornichons (see page 141)

1 Place veal in a heavy-based saucepan or enamelled cast-iron casserole just large enough to fit all the ingredients. Cover veal with onion, tuna, bay leaves, 2 anchovy fillets and half of the capers. Tip in the verjuice or dry white wine, 75 ml of the olive oil and up to 375 ml water, adding just enough liquid to immerse veal during cooking. Bring to a simmer, then cover, reduce heat to low and cook at a gentle simmer for 1 hour (use a simmer mat if necessary). Remove pan from heat and leave meat to cool completely in its juices.

2 Once cooled, remove meat and set aside, discarding bay leaves. Strain cooking liquid, reserving both solids and liquid. Press solids with 1 cup (250 ml) of the strained cooking liquid through a sieve or food mill (or blend in a food processor and then sieve it). Set aside.

3 Using a mortar and pestle, smash the hard-boiled egg yolks to a paste with a dash of lemon juice, then add raw egg yolk (this could also be done carefully in a food processor). Slowly add remaining olive oil drop by drop, incorporating it into the mayonnaise as you go, then add 1 cup (250 ml) of the sieved sauce. Check for seasoning and acidity, adding more lemon juice if required.

4 Slice veal very thinly, making sure you cut across the grain, then overlap on a platter. Cover with mayonnaise. Cut remaining anchovies into strips and arrange in a criss-cross pattern over the mayonnaise. Place remaining capers in the centre of each 'diamond'. Serve at room temperature with thinly sliced lemon and cornichons.

Middle

Roast Barossa chook with preserved lemon and tarragon butter

When I cook chicken, I never use anything other than a well-brought-up chook: the texture and flavour are so different from that of a mass-produced bird you wonder whether they are even of the same species. There is little point buying a free-range chook under two kilograms: the smaller birds haven't had the time to develop in texture and flavour.

1 × 2 kg Barossa or other well-brought-up chook
125 g unsalted butter, softened and chopped
2 small quarters preserved lemon (see page 141),
    flesh removed, rind rinsed and finely chopped
⅓ cup (4 tablespoons) French tarragon leaves
2 cloves garlic, crushed
2½ tablespoons extra virgin olive oil
sea salt and freshly ground black pepper
½ cup (125 ml) verjuice (see page 141)
1 cup (250 ml) Golden Chicken Stock
    (see page 132), warmed

1 Remove chook from refrigerator and bring to room temperature, if you have time.

2 Preheat fan-forced oven to 200°C (220°C).

3 Place butter, preserved lemon and tarragon in a food processor and whiz to combine; don't over-process or the butter will split. Place chook breast-side up on a trivet in a shallow roasting pan or baking dish (mine is 5 cm deep). Use your hands to separate skin from flesh, working from the legs, then up and across both breasts. Tuck wings underneath chook. Place garlic in the cavity. Push butter mixture under skin with your fingertips. Mix olive oil with a good pinch of salt and pepper and massage into skin. Cover breast only with foil.

4 Place roasting pan on middle shelf of oven and roast chook for 40 minutes. Remove foil from breast and use to cover legs. Pour verjuice over chicken and roast for a further 20–30 minutes or until cooked.

5 Remove chook from oven and place breast-side down on the trivet to rest for 40 minutes, loosely covered with foil.

6 Meanwhile, for the jus, pour pan juices and warm chicken stock into a narrow serving jug, then refrigerate while chook is resting. Just before serving, scoop away and discard any fat that has risen to the top, then warm the jus.

7 Carve the chook, then pour over the jus. Serve with your choice of salad or vegetables.

Chicken braised with figs, honey and vinegar

Here is another of those one-pot dishes that your family and friends will love. The trick is to use a shallow baking dish so that the ingredients come almost to the top of the dish; that way, when you drizzle the chicken skin with honey it will caramelise beautifully as so much more of it is exposed to the heat than if cooked in a deeper dish.

extra virgin olive oil, for cooking
2 red onions, roughly chopped
2 teaspoons chopped lemon thyme
2 teaspoons chopped rosemary
4 large ripe figs, halved
4 large Barossa or other corn-fed chicken
    marylands (thigh and drumstick joints),
    thighs and drumsticks separated
sea salt
1 cinnamon stick
½ cup (125 ml) Golden Chicken Stock
    (see page 132)
½ cup (125 ml) verjuice (see page 141)
2 tablespoons sherry vinegar (see page 141)
zest of 1 lemon, removed in thin strips with
    a vegetable peeler, leaving the bitter pith
2 tablespoons honey
chopped flat-leaf parsley (optional) and
    Grilled Semolina (optional, see page 139),
    to serve

1 Preheat fan-forced oven to 200°C (220°C).

2 Heat a splash of olive oil in a frying pan over medium heat, then add onion, thyme and rosemary and saute for 5 minutes or until softened. Transfer to a shallow flameproof baking dish. Quickly saute fig halves in the frying pan and transfer to onion mixture in baking dish.

3 Sprinkle chicken pieces with salt and place on top of onion and figs, then add cinnamon, stock, verjuice, vinegar and lemon zest. Drizzle with honey, then bake for 30–35 minutes or until chicken is cooked, basting occasionally with pan juices. Remove from oven and transfer chicken and figs to a dish to rest; keep warm. Remove cinnamon stick, if desired. Simmer pan juices over high heat until reduced and syrupy.

4 Return chicken and figs to sauce, then drizzle with olive oil and scatter with parsley, if using. Serve at once with grilled semolina, if desired.

Honey and lemon chicken drummettes

Whilst I love making this dish with my grandchildren, this doesn't mean that I see it as just a 'children's meal' – I've never known any adults to refuse these tasty little morsels. Although I usually bake them, the drummettes could be cooked on a barbecue too; just turn the chicken frequently to prevent the honey from burning. Don't forget to leave the drummettes to rest a little before serving to maximise their flavour and moistness.

Chicken drummettes are the small drumsticks attached to the wing bones. If you can't buy them separately, buy whole wings instead (with the wing tips removed) and cut them in two at the joint.

½ cup (180 g) honey, warmed
1 tablespoon roughly chopped lemon thyme,
    plus extra to serve (optional)
¼ cup (60 ml) extra virgin olive oil
1 tablespoon finely grated lemon zest
⅓ cup (80 ml) lemon juice
1 kg chicken drummettes
sea salt

1 Mix honey, thyme, olive oil, lemon zest and lemon juice together, then use to marinate drummettes in the refrigerator for 20 minutes.

2 Preheat fan-forced oven to 220°C (240°C).

3 Season chicken drummettes with salt, then place on a baking tray in one layer and bake for 15 minutes or until cooked through, turning halfway through cooking.

4 Leave chicken drummettes to rest for 5 minutes, then serve scattered with extra lemon thyme leaves, if desired.

Coq au vin

After trying coq au vin more than a decade ago, I wondered what all the fuss was about. Now I know it's all about starting with a really good chook and decent wine (no vin ordinaire here, please), and allowing the time. For a peasant dish, this requires attention to detail, but the result is outstanding.

1 × 2.6 kg free-range chicken or cockerel,
    jointed into 8 pieces
1 tablespoon extra virgin olive oil
40 g unsalted butter, softened
100 g salt pork, rind removed,
    flesh cut into 2.5 cm pieces
24 pickling onions, peeled with
    root ends intact
18 mushrooms, trimmed
2 carrots, finely chopped
2 sticks celery, finely chopped
2 sprigs thyme
5 fresh bay leaves
¼ cup (60 ml) brandy
1½ cups (375 ml) very reduced veal stock
1 tablespoon plain flour
flat-leaf parsley leaves (optional), to serve

MARINADE
2 cloves garlic, thinly sliced
1 onion, thinly sliced
2 sprigs thyme
3 cups (750 ml) red wine

1 For the marinade, mix garlic, onion, thyme and red wine in a large bowl. Add chicken and marinate overnight or for at least 8 hours. Remove chicken from marinade just before cooking and reserve marinade.

2 Preheat fan-forced oven to 150°C (170°C).

3 Heat olive oil and 20 g butter in an enamelled cast-iron casserole over medium heat until foamy. Saute salt pork until browned, then remove with a slotted spoon. Gently seal chicken, taking care not to burn butter. Remove and set aside. Toss onions in pan until slightly coloured, then set aside. Repeat with mushrooms and set aside. Add carrot, celery, thyme and bay leaves and cook until lightly caramelised.

4 Return chicken and salt pork to pan, then gently stir through carrot, celery and herbs. Warm brandy in a small saucepan, then carefully light with a match, wait for alcohol to burn off and pour over chicken. Pour in stock and 1½ cups (375 ml) reserved marinade and slowly bring to a simmer over low heat. Cover and cook in oven for 1½ hours. Leave to cool completely, then refrigerate.

5 Before serving, preheat oven to 150°C fan-forced (170°C). Remove fat from surface, then add onions and mushrooms. Reheat in oven (or over low heat for 30 minutes using a simmer mat). Remove the meat and vegetables and keep warm. Strain cooking liquor, then cover chicken to keep warm. Bring cooking liquor to a boil and reduce a little. Make a paste with the flour and remaining butter and whisk small amounts into sauce over heat to thicken it. Simmer for a further 10 minutes until sauce is lightly thickened with a glossy sheen. Pour sauce over chicken, sprinkle with parsley leaves (if using) and serve.

Steeping grilled quail in a fresh marinade is a technique I've long loved – the beauty of it is that the flavourings can be altered according to what you have to hand. Instead of dried figs, you could add grapes and roasted walnuts, or perhaps raisins that have been reconstituted in red-wine vinegar and then tossed in nut-brown butter with some rosemary. A recipe is just an idea, after all.

8 quail
extra virgin olive oil, for drizzling
freshly ground black pepper

FIG BATH
8 tiny white or 4 larger dried figs
verjuice (see page 141), for drizzling
2 lemons
½ cup (125 ml) extra virgin olive oil
large handful basil leaves
freshly ground black pepper

1 Using kitchen shears, cut away backbone from each quail and slip out rib cage with your fingers. Rub each bird with a little olive oil, then season with pepper and set aside for 1 hour before grilling.

2 Meanwhile, preheat a barbecue or prepare your fire, allowing it to burn down to glowing embers.

3 Start to prepare the fig bath by reconstituting figs in enough verjuice to cover them for 20 minutes, then drain and cut them in half (or quarters, if using larger figs).

4 Remove zest from lemons using a vegetable peeler, leaving white pith, then juice 1 lemon. Set aside.

5 Grill quail, turning frequently, for about 8 minutes in all, depending on the heat of the fire. While quail are cooking, finish preparing the fig bath by pouring olive oil into a shallow glass dish, then adding figs, lemon zest and juice. Chop basil finely and add to bath with a good grinding of pepper. Transfer cooked quail to fig bath and rest for 10 minutes, turning once or twice, before serving.

Quince-glazed quail

SERVES 6

I like to serve this with grilled polenta, but soft polenta or waxy potatoes such as my favourites, Nicolas, are fine too. A salad of bitter greens, such as witlof, radicchio and rocket, is the perfect accompaniment.

40 g quince paste
squeeze of lemon juice
extra virgin olive oil, for cooking
1 small onion, finely chopped
3 super-thin slices round pancetta,
  finely chopped
1 tablespoon finely chopped rosemary
50 g unsalted butter, chopped
100 g chicken livers
¼ cup (40 g) pine nuts
30 g fresh white breadcrumbs
sea salt and freshly ground black pepper
6 jumbo quail (about 200 g each)
rocket leaves, to serve

1 Melt quince paste with ½ cup (125 ml) water and lemon juice in a small saucepan over low heat, stirring until smooth and lump-free; take care not to burn paste. Set aside.

2 Heat a splash of olive oil in a frying pan over low–medium heat, then saute onion, pancetta and rosemary for 6–8 minutes or until just tender. Transfer to a bowl and set aside.

3 Heat 25 g butter and a splash of olive oil in the same pan over medium–high heat. When butter foams, add livers and cook for 1 minute on each side or until just coloured on outside but still pink on inside. Remove from pan and leave to cool slightly. Trim livers, then cut into large pieces, discarding any connective tissue, and add to onion mixture. Add pine nuts and breadcrumbs and stir gently to combine.

4 Preheat a fan-forced oven to 220°C (240°C).

5 Season cavity of each quail with salt and pepper. Divide breadcrumb mixture equally among quail and carefully fill each cavity. Tuck wings underneath quail. Secure quail legs together with a toothpick or tie with kitchen string (see photo opposite) to enclose filling. Season quail with salt.

6 Heat remaining butter in a clean large frying pan over medium heat, then, when it's foaming, gently brown quail on all sides. Place quail on a baking tray, breast-side up, then brush quince glaze generously over each one; if glaze is too hard to spread, gently reheat over low heat.

7 Roast quail for 10–12 minutes or until cooked through; do not overcook. Leave to rest, breast-side down, in a warm place for 10–15 minutes. Serve with rocket leaves.

Roasted pheasant with sage, orange and juniper berries

These cooking times are approximate. Translating the time achieved when using a commercial oven to that required by a domestic oven is precariously difficult. Domestic ovens vary greatly in their ability to heat evenly and to recover the heat once the door has been opened. The breast should feel firm and yet yield to a soft squeeze when it is ready.

handful loosely packed sage leaves
80 g unsalted butter, softened
1 × 1 kg pheasant
1 orange
20 juniper berries
2 teaspoons finely chopped marjoram
2 teaspoons finely chopped thyme
½ cup (125 ml) reduced Golden Chicken
**   Stock (see page 132)**
sea salt and freshly ground black pepper

1 Preheat fan-forced oven to 200°C (220°C).

2 Spread sage leaves on a baking tray and dot with 40 g butter. Bake for 12 minutes until crisp and nut-brown, then set aside.

3 Increase oven temperature to 230°C fan-forced (250°C).

4 Cut legs away from pheasant, then cut along either side of backbone and discard it. 'Spatchcock' the bird by flattening it out. Remove zest from half the orange with a vegetable peeler, leaving white pith, then juice the orange. Place pheasant legs and flattened-out breast in a baking dish, skin-side up. Smear pheasant with remaining butter, then pour over orange juice and sprinkle on juniper berries, marjoram, thyme and zest.

5 Roast pheasant for 12 minutes, then reduce oven temperature to 180°C fan-forced (200°C) and cook for a further 12 minutes. Remove legs from baking dish, then turn breast over and return it to oven for a further 2 minutes. Check it is cooked by inserting a skewer into the meatiest part – if the juices run clear or a faint pink, the bird is ready. Remove from oven and rest, breast-side down, for at least 8 minutes. Strain juices from baking dish into a small saucepan and add reduced chicken stock. Bring to a boil and check for seasoning.

6 Carve breast away from bone and serve with legs, drizzled with reduced stock and topped with the crisped sage leaves and orange zest.

Five-spice barbecued duck with morello cherry spoon sweets

This dish came about one lazy Sunday afternoon when we had the family around for a late lunch/ early dinner. Nothing could have been simpler, and the fatty skin of the Pekin duck 'basted' the meat as it grilled. This dish will not be successful unless Pekin ducks are used, as other breeds will not have enough fat for the cooking method used here.

2 x 1.2 kg Pekin ducks
2½ teaspoons Chinese five-spice powder
Morello Cherry Spoon Sweets (see page 136)
    and bitter green salad, to serve

1 Cut drumsticks and thighs away from each duck in one piece, then cut away each breast. Cut drumsticks away from thighs and remove thigh bones. Freeze drumsticks for another dish. Sprinkle duck breasts and thighs with Chinese five-spice powder and rub in well.

2 Preheat a barbecue grill plate to high – if you are using a wood-fired grill, make sure the fire has burnt down to glowing embers, then remove some of the red-hot coals. (The idea is to seal the duck over high heat without burning the skin, then finish cooking the meat over a more mellow heat.) Seal breasts and thigh meat quickly on open grill side, rotating to achieve a criss-cross pattern on the skin. Transfer duck to coolest corner of the barbecue plate and cook thigh meat for 15 minutes on each side. (As breasts only need 6–7 minutes a side, add them to the hot plate when you turn the thigh meat. After 6–7 minutes a side the breast meat will still be pink – you can cook them for a longer time, if you prefer.) Remove duck from heat and rest in a warm spot for 8 minutes.

3 Serve with cherry spoon sweets and a bitter green salad.

Roast leg of Suffolk lamb

I've loved Suffolk lamb ever since I was introduced to it in the 1980s by a farmer in Mallala. I was blown away by the difference in taste and texture and hooked from that moment on. Not that it was easy to procure, until Richard Gunner of Coorong Angus fame started to breed Suffolk lambs. Nowadays, John and Jan Angas of Angaston sell their Suffolk lamb at the Barossa Markets every Saturday morning. This succulent lamb goes particularly well with green-olive tapenade and creamy labna.

1 × 3 kg leg lamb (I use Suffolk lamb)
3 cloves garlic, sliced lengthways
    into 4
3 sprigs rosemary, leaves picked
    and finely chopped
¼ cup (60 ml) extra virgin olive oil
2 tablespoons sea salt
½ cup (125 ml) verjuice (see page 141)
rosemary sprigs (optional), to serve

1 Remove lamb from refrigerator 2 hours before cooking to come to room temperature.

2 Preheat fan-forced oven to 180°C (200°C).

3 Make 12 incisions in skin evenly over surface of lamb and insert garlic slices. Combine rosemary and olive oil and rub all over lamb skin. Rub liberally with salt.

4 Place lamb in a roasting pan and roast for 30 minutes. Reduce oven temperature to 160°C fan-forced (180°C). Turn lamb leg over and cook for another 20 minutes. Turn lamb leg over again and cook for another 30 minutes. Turn oven off and leave lamb in oven for 30 minutes with the door ajar.

5 Remove lamb from oven and leave to rest for another 30 minutes. Meanwhile, pour pan juices into a tall jug and refrigerate the juices to solidify the fat so it can be skimmed from surface. Remove fat from pan juices, then place juices and verjuice in a saucepan and reduce over high heat to serve as a jus.

6 Serve with lamb jus, garnished with rosemary sprigs, if desired.

Lamb moussaka

My friend Peter Wall often cooks dinner for us, especially on the frequent occasions when I've been travelling and arrive home jetlagged. His moussaka is a favourite. It is lighter than any I'd eaten so I coaxed the recipe from him. Peter's secret is to use good chicken stock in the bechamel sauce.

extra virgin olive oil, for cooking
1 onion, finely chopped
1 clove garlic, crushed
500 g minced lamb
1 cm piece cinnamon stick, pounded
sea salt
½ cup (125 ml) red wine
1 tablespoon tomato paste (puree)
1 cup (250 ml) Tomato Sugo (see page 135)
    or tomato passata
finely grated zest of 1 lemon
2½ tablespoons chopped lemon thyme
3 eggplants (aubergines), cut into
    1.5 cm-thick slices
1 quantity Bechamel Sauce (see page 135)
¼ cup (25 g) grated Parmigiano Reggiano
¼ cup (15 g) fresh breadcrumbs
1 tablespoon rinsed and finely chopped
    preserved lemon rind

1 Heat a splash of olive oil in a large saucepan over low heat and saute onion for 5 minutes, then add garlic and cook for another 5 minutes. Push onion and garlic to one side of pan, then brown lamb with cinnamon in batches over high heat, breaking up any lumps with the back of a wooden spoon and season with salt. Return all meat to pan, then add wine, tomato paste and tomato sugo or passata. Stir to combine and bring to the boil. Add lemon zest and 2 tablespoons lemon thyme and simmer over low heat for 20 minutes.

2 Preheat fan-forced oven to 200°C (220°C).

3 Brush eggplant with olive oil, then cook on a hot chargrill pan over high heat until golden on both sides. Lightly grease a 1 litre-capacity baking dish with olive oil. Place a layer of eggplant in the base, then add a layer of lamb mixture. Repeat layering process until all eggplant and lamb mixture are used, finishing with an eggplant layer. Pour bechamel sauce over eggplant.

4 Mix together Parmigiano, breadcrumbs, preserved lemon and remaining lemon thyme and generously sprinkle over bechamel. Bake moussaka for 30 minutes or until top is golden. Serve at once.

Spaghetti bolognese my way

Whilst you don't have to follow my lead and add chicken livers to your spaghetti bolognese, they're the jewel in the crown for me. The trick to cooking this is to saute the meat in batches so that each batch is really well browned. The addition of red wine is essential as it really adds another level of richness. I've given 20 to 25 minutes as the cooking time, but the real test as to whether it is ready is the colour – the amalgamation of the meat, tomato paste and red wine should lead to a deep, richly coloured result.

extra virgin olive oil, for cooking
1 small onion, roughly chopped
2 cloves garlic, crushed
2 tablespoons finely chopped oregano
200 g chicken livers
500 g minced beef
sea salt
500 g minced pork
280 g tomato paste (puree)
300 ml red wine
½ cup (125 ml) Golden Chicken Stock
    (see page 132), veal stock or Vegetable
    Stock (see page 132)
2 tablespoons finely chopped thyme
2 small fresh bay leaves
500 g spaghetti
freshly ground black pepper
chopped flat-leaf parsley, to serve

1 Heat a splash of olive oil in a saucepan over medium heat and saute onion and garlic for 10 minutes or until translucent, then add oregano. Transfer to a bowl and set aside. Add livers to pan and cook for 30 seconds on both sides or until coloured, then remove and leave to cool. Remove connective tissue, then cut livers into pieces and set aside.

2 Add another splash of olive oil to the pan and add minced beef in batches, then season with salt and saute until browned. Add minced pork in batches and cook until browned. Return onion mixture to pan, then add tomato paste and cook over low heat for 10 minutes. Add wine, stock, thyme and bay leaves, then bring to a simmer and cook for 20–25 minutes or longer if needed. Add livers to bolognese mixture 5 minutes before serving.

3 Meanwhile, cook spaghetti in a large saucepan of boiling salted water according to manufacturers' instructions, and have warm plates or bowls ready to serve.

4 Season bolognese with pepper, then serve with drained spaghetti and a generous scattering of chopped parsley.

How I loved the amazing White Rocks veal chops from Western Australia that used to grace the table at Stephanie's. That extraordinary restaurant is a part of history now, but my memories of sitting at a window table eating that veal have never been surpassed. Thankfully, White Rocks veal is still going strong, and Vince Garreffa of Mondo di Carne, Perth's master butcher, is happy to mail-order.

extra virgin olive oil, for cooking
1 tablespoon finely chopped rosemary
¼ teaspoon freshly ground black pepper
6 × 2 cm-thick veal cutlets, French-trimmed
50 g unsalted butter
2 tablespoons lemon juice
steamed green beans, green salad and baby
    potatoes rolled in butter and chopped
    flat-leaf parsley (optional), to serve

1 Rub olive oil, rosemary and pepper into veal and leave for 10 minutes for the flavours to infuse.

2 Melt butter in a frying pan over medium heat until nut-brown and foaming. Pan-fry cutlets for 6 minutes on one side, then turn and cook for another 4 minutes on other side for medium. (The cooking time will depend on the thickness of the veal.) Transfer veal to a plate and leave to rest for at least 5 minutes. Pour lemon juice into pan to deglaze, then drizzle over veal.

3 Serve veal with steamed green beans, a green salad and boiled baby potatoes rolled in melted butter and chopped flat-leaf parsley, if desired.

Coorong Angus beef pies with red wine, fennel and green olives

SERVES 8

I like to slowly braise the meat in a crockpot but it could easily be cooked in an enamelled cast-iron casserole over low heat with a simmer mat or in a 120°C fan-forced (140°C) oven for a few hours.

plain flour, for dusting
sea salt and freshly ground black pepper
1 kg Coorong Angus Beef chuck, or other
    quality beef chuck, cut into 3 cm cubes
extra virgin olive oil, for cooking
400 ml shiraz
1 medium–large bulb fennel, trimmed and
    finely chopped
16 golden shallots, peeled
4 cloves garlic, chopped
2 cups (500 ml) veal stock or Golden
    Chicken Stock (see page 132)
1 sprig rosemary
6 sprigs thyme
2 fresh bay leaves
finely grated zest of 1 orange
16 green olives, pitted
1 quantity Sour-cream Pastry (see page 138)
1 egg, beaten

1 Season flour with salt and pepper, then toss meat in seasoned flour, shaking off any excess. Working in batches, seal meat in olive oil in a large, deep frying pan over high heat until all meat is browned.

2 Heat a crockpot to its highest setting, then add meat. Deglaze frying pan with wine, reducing it by three-quarters over high heat, then add wine to crockpot. Return frying pan to medium heat, then add more olive oil and saute fennel and shallots for 6–8 minutes or until soft. Add garlic and saute for another 5 minutes, then transfer vegetables to crockpot. Add stock to frying pan, bring to a rapid boil over high heat, then add to crockpot with herbs. Cook on highest setting for 30 minutes, then turn to lowest setting and cook for 6 hours (or even overnight) or until meat is melt-in-the-mouth tender, adding orange zest and olives in the last 20 minutes. If juices haven't reduced and become syrupy, strain into a small saucepan, then simmer over high heat until reduced. Return to beef mixture and stir to coat. Let beef mixture cool.

3 Roll pastry on a floured bench to 5 mm thick, then cut to fit bases of 8 individual pie tins, making sure pastry overhangs the lips of the pie tins. Brush bases with beaten egg to help seal in the juices. Cut out pastry tops to fit.

4 Divide beef mixture among pie tins and cover with pastry tops. Fold edges of pastry tops to seal, then brush tops with beaten egg. Chill pies in fridge up to 1 day in advance, or, if short of time, pop in freezer for 10 minutes.

5 Preheat a fan-forced oven to 220°C (240°). Place pie tins on a baking tray and bake for 20 minutes or until golden brown. Serve.

There's a lot of variation in the quality of corned meat you can buy, so buy from a butcher you trust. The range of cooking times and resulting texture needed can be extreme.

¼ cup (60 ml) olive oil
3 onions, roughly chopped
2 cloves garlic, roughly chopped
1½ tablespoons brown sugar
½ cup (125 ml) verjuice (see page 141)
3 fresh bay leaves
1 teaspoon black peppercorns
1 × 1.2 kg corned silverside (with a good amount
    of fat), brought to room temperature
boiling water, to cover
Bechamel Sauce with a spoonful of mustard
    stirred through (optional, see page 135),
    to serve

SUGARLOAF CABBAGE
2 teaspoons caraway seeds
1 quarter preserved lemon, flesh removed,
    rind rinsed and thinly sliced
¼ cup (60 ml) extra virgin olive oil
1 kg sugarloaf or savoy cabbage, outer leaves
    and core discarded, remaining leaves cut
    into 2 cm thick slices
sea salt and freshly ground black pepper
¼ cup (60 ml) verjuice (see page 141)
small handful roughly chopped flat-leaf
    parsley (optional)

1 Heat 2 tablespoons of the olive oil over medium heat in a heavy-based casserole just large enough to fit the silverside. Add onion and cook for 10 minutes, stirring occasionally until golden brown. Add garlic and cook for 1 minute, then add brown sugar. Pour in verjuice and bring to a sizzling bubble. Add bay leaves and peppercorns.

2 Meanwhile, heat remaining olive oil in a heavy-based frying pan over medium–high heat. Add silverside, fat-side down, and cook for 3 minutes or until golden brown. Transfer meat to casserole, fat-side up. Add just enough boiling water to cover meat, then bring to the boil over high heat. Reduce heat to low–medium, cover with the lid and simmer for 1¼ hours (if you have a meat thermometer, the internal temperature should register 70°C). Transfer to a plate, then cover loosely with foil and leave to rest for 20 minutes.

3 For the sugarloaf cabbage, toast caraway seeds in a small frying pan over medium heat for 1½–2 minutes or until aromatic and light golden, then set aside. Soak preserved lemon rind in a small bowl of cold water for 10 minutes, then drain. Heat olive oil in a large heavy-based frying pan over medium–high heat and gradually add cabbage. Cook for 5 minutes, stirring until it starts to become tender, then season with salt and pepper. Add verjuice and increase heat to high, then simmer for 1 minute or until verjuice is syrupy. Remove pan from heat and scatter with caraway seeds, preserved lemon and parsley (if using), then transfer to a serving bowl.

4 Serve slices of silverside with bechamel sauce, if desired, and sugarloaf cabbage.

I owe the idea for this recipe to Salvatore Pepe of Adelaide restaurant Cibo. Having first tasted this dish there, I took the principle of it, but instead of using a mouth-watering fillet of beef like Salvatore, I've used a thick slice from the back cut of rump. Drizzling the meat with balsamic or vino cotto during the critical resting period adds something special. It is also crucial to carve the steak against the grain. This is a great way to serve a perfect piece of beef.

1 × 450 g (2.5 cm thick) piece rump (I use Coorong
    Angus beef tender-stretched rump)
2 stalks rosemary, leaves picked and chopped
extra virgin olive oil, for cooking
sea salt
¼ cup (60 ml) vino cotto (see page 141) or
    balsamic vinegar, plus extra for drizzling
freshly ground black pepper
100 g Parmigiano Reggiano, shaved
generous bunch of rocket leaves, to serve

1 Take beef out of the refrigerator 1 hour before you plan to cook it to bring to room temperature.

2 Rub beef with rosemary and olive oil, then season with salt. Cook on a very hot char-grill plate for about 2 minutes on each side, then turn on its edge to cook the fat for a couple of minutes; the idea is to sear it quickly over really high heat. Reduce heat to medium and cook for 3–4 minutes for medium–rare.

3 Transfer to a serving plate, splash with vino cotto or balsamic and a little more olive oil and leave to rest for about 8 minutes (that is, double the cooking time). Season with salt and pepper, then carve against the grain into thick slices.

4 Serve beef drizzled with a little more vino cotto or balsamic and olive oil, with shaved Parmigiano and rocket leaves alongside.

Beef tagine with dried fruit

Whilst tagines are cooked every day in Morocco, for me the robust flavours make this is a winter dish. Although this can be served as soon as it's cooked, its flavour improves if made a day or two in advance.

1.5 kg oyster blade steak, cut into 4 cm pieces
1 tablespoon ras el hanout (see page 141)
¼ cup (40 g) raw almonds
extra virgin olive oil, for cooking
1 large onion, roughly chopped
2 cloves garlic, chopped
4 saffron threads
sea salt and freshly ground black pepper
1 large cinnamon stick
4 beef marrow bones or 4 osso bucco
24 dried apricots
18 large prunes, pitted
2 teaspoons rosewater
¼ cup (55 g) brown sugar
chopped flat-leaf parsley and couscous
    or freekeh, to serve

1 Mix beef and ras el hanout together, cover with plastic film and leave to marinate at room temperature for 1 hour.

2 Preheat fan-forced oven to 180°C (200°C). Roast almonds for 8–10 minutes or until golden, then cool. Reduce oven temperature to 150°C fan-forced (170°C).

3 Heat a splash of olive oil in a heavy-based frying pan over low–medium heat and saute onion and garlic for 6–8 minutes or until translucent. Add saffron, then transfer to a large enamelled cast-iron casserole or tagine with a tight-fitting lid and set aside. Heat a little more olive oil in the pan, then brown meat in batches, seasoning with salt and pepper as you go. Add beef, cinnamon, marrow bones and ¼ cup (60 ml) water to casserole. Cover and cook in oven for 1 hour.

4 Meanwhile, put apricots, prunes, rosewater and brown sugar into a small saucepan and add just enough water to cover fruit. Bring to the boil, then reduce heat to low and simmer for 10 minutes or until fruit plumps up. (The fruit will absorb almost all of the liquid.)

5 After meat has cooked for 1 hour, add dried fruit mixture and stir to combine. Cook for another 45–60 minutes or until meat is tender but not falling apart. If there is a lot of liquid, remove meat and fruit from pan and reduce liquid over high heat until a little syrupy. Return meat and fruit to pan and season to taste, if necessary, then warm through.

6 Scatter almonds and parsley over the tagine. Top each serve with some cooked marrow spooned out of the bones. Serve with couscous or freekeh.

My Italian beef 'daube'

During a trip to Italy, my friend Ann Parronchi took me to the terracotta kilns in Chianti where workmen used to cook beef shins overnight in the residual heat of the kiln. This is my interpretation of what that dish may have been like. If I make this when globe artichokes are in season, I like to braise them in verjuice to serve alongside, as I did when this was photographed.

1 beef shin (off the bone), sinew and
    excess fat discarded
2 sticks celery, diced
1 carrot, diced
1 onion, roughly chopped
1 small leek, white part only,
    roughly chopped
6 sprigs thyme
4 stalks flat-leaf parsley
1 fresh bay leaf
800 ml veal or beef stock
400 ml red wine
softened unsalted butter
plain flour, for dusting
32 golden shallots, peeled
2 heads garlic, cloves of 1 head peeled,
    second head halved widthways
zest of 1 orange, removed in thin strips with
    a vegetable peeler, leaving white pith
1 cup (160 g) kalamata olives
sea salt and freshly ground black pepper
soft polenta or mashed potato, to serve

MARINADE
2 cups (500 ml) extra virgin olive oil
zest of 1 orange, removed in a thin strip with
    a vegetable peeler, leaving the bitter pith
1 fresh bay leaf
1 sprig rosemary
1 sprig thyme
several stalks flat-leaf parsley

1 For the marinade, place olive oil, zest and herbs in a large glass bowl. Add the beef and turn to coat, then cover with plastic film and leave to marinate overnight (if marinating during the day, turn the meat frequently to ensure it remains moist and evenly exposed to the flavourings).

2 Using a little olive oil from the marinade, gently seal the shin in a frying pan over low heat, then transfer the shin to an enamelled cast-iron casserole. Add celery, carrot, onion and leek. Tie thyme and parsley with kitchen string and add to the pot with bay leaf. Cover with veal stock and red wine and bring to a simmer. Reduce heat to a very gentle simmer, then cover with the lid and cook for 8 hours, turning several times until meat is tender to the touch and sinews are like jelly. (Alternatively, cook in oven at 140°C fan-forced [160°C] for the same length of time.) The cooking juices will benefit from being reduced and thickened. Make a paste with equal quantities of butter and flour – you will need 30 g paste to every 250 ml cooking juices. Remove meat from cooking liquor, cover and set aside. Bring liquor to a fast simmer and reduce a little. Slowly whisk in small amounts of paste at a time to thicken the sauce. Reduce heat to low and return meat to casserole.

3 Meanwhile, preheat fan-forced oven to 200°C (220°C). Melt a knob of butter in a flameproof baking dish Add shallots and garlic and toss to coat. Transfer to oven and roast for 30 minutes or until shallots and garlic have caramelised. Set aside.

4 An hour before the 'daube' is due to finish cooking, add orange zest, olives, shallots and garlic to casserole and continue to cook. When cooked, season with salt and pepper and serve in a warmed dish with polenta or mashed potato.

Roast Berkshire pork belly with verjuice and Seville marmalade glaze

A love for pork has only come to me in the last 15 years or so. Until my time in Italy with Stephanie, other than the occasional bit of bacon, I disliked pork intensely. During that trip, however, I found that pork could be ambrosial, depending on the breed and feed. Now, thanks to my daughter Saskia, who breeds Berkshire pigs, I am lucky to have a ready supply of heritage-breed pork virtually on my doorstep.

1 large clove garlic, chopped
1 teaspoon sea salt, plus extra as needed
1 tablespoon minced ginger
⅓ cup (115 g) Seville marmalade
2 tablespoons verjuice (see page 141)
2 tablespoons extra virgin olive oil
1 × 2 kg pork belly (I use Berkshire pork),
  skin removed
1 tablespoon freshly ground black pepper
rapini (optional) or other green vegetable,
  to serve

1 Using the flat of a large knife blade, crush garlic and salt to form a paste. Combine garlic paste, ginger, marmalade, verjuice and olive oil in a bowl to make the glaze.

2 Place pork belly in a roasting pan and season with salt and pepper. Pour glaze evenly over pork and stand for 10 minutes.

3 Meanwhile, preheat fan-forced oven to 120°C (140°C).

4 Roast pork for 3 hours or until tender and well-glazed. Serve with rapini (a peppery green vegetable that tastes somewhere between turnip and broccoli) or any other robustly flavoured green vegetable.

Pickled pork with pickled quince

This is the meal that my late mother-in-law served when welcoming me into her family. It's such an important Beer family dish that it finds its way onto my table in any season. As Flo would have known, the pork must be fatty or you shouldn't bother. You don't have to eat all the fat, but without it you won't have the flavour. The pickled quince saves the dish from being too rich. Delicious hot, this is also good served cold (some would even say better), which means that it is always included in the line-up at Christmas in our house.

1 × 1.3 kg hand of pickled pork
1 cup (250 ml) white-wine vinegar
2 onions, peeled and cut into quarters
1 teaspoon black or white peppercorns
2 fresh bay leaves
12 pieces Flo Beer's Pickled Quince
   (see page 136) or other pickled fruit

1 Put pickled pork into a large heavy-based stainless-steel stockpot and pour in vinegar and 3.5 litres water. Add onion, peppercorns and bay leaves to pot, then bring to a simmer. Stand pot on a simmer mat and simmer very slowly for 3 hours. Allow pork to cool in cooking liquor.

2 Slice meat and arrange on a platter with the onion, a little of the cooking liquor and the pickled quince, then serve.

Tripe with surprise peas, verjuice and pancetta

When we decided to do a segment on tripe for the TV series *The Cook and the Chef* I wanted to show the potential of combining it with different flavours. We set up a stall at the Barossa Farmer's Market one Saturday morning to see if anyone was game to try it. We got a great reaction as most people loved the dish. The most delightful thing of all was the number of children who tasted it and loved it – you couldn't fake a child's reaction if you tried, and there for all to see were these youngsters hoeing in and coming back for more!

1 kg honeycomb tripe (ask your butcher
    for partially cooked tripe)
20 g unsalted butter
extra virgin olive oil, for cooking
8 small leeks, white part only,
    sliced into rings
1½ cups (375 ml) verjuice (see page 141)
2 tablespoons chopped lemon thyme
3 cups (750 ml) Golden Chicken Stock
    (see page 132)
sea salt and freshly ground black pepper
1 cup (120 g) Surprise peas (available
    from larger supermarkets)
12 thin slices pancetta

1 Soak tripe in cold water for 30 minutes before cooking. Drain and dry thoroughly, then cut into 3 cm × 2 cm strips.

2 Heat butter in a large saucepan over medium–high heat until nut-brown, add a dash of olive oil to prevent burning, then add tripe and seal on all sides until well coloured. Remove tripe and set aside. Add leek and cook for 10 minutes or until leek is just soft. Return tripe to pan. Deglaze pan with verjuice over high heat, then add lemon thyme and chicken stock and season to taste with salt and pepper.

3 Reduce heat to low, then simmer gently, covered with a tight-fitting lid, for 1¼ hours. Add peas and cook over high heat for another 30 minutes or until liquid is reduced and syrupy. Adjust seasoning if desired.

4 Meanwhile, preheat fan-forced oven to 200°C (220°C). Lay pancetta on a baking tray and bake for 10 minutes or until crisp. Garnish tripe with crisp pancetta and serve.

Spicy pork and apple pasties

I had great fun putting together my take on the pasty, a South Australian favourite. I decided it would be fun to take a different slant on the traditional concept of a pasty, one version of which contained meat at one end and apple, for dessert, at the other. I incorporated the apple with the meat, then added currants and pine nuts for a Sicilian touch, creating pasties that are full of flavour.

⅓ cup (50 g) pine nuts
½ cup (125 ml) verjuice (see page 141)
¼ cup (35 g) dried currants
⅓ cup (30 g) dried apples, chopped
extra virgin olive oil, for cooking
1 small onion, finely chopped
2 cloves garlic, finely chopped
3 teaspoons ground ginger
3 teaspoons ground cinnamon
2 tablespoons honey
500 g minced pork
¼ preserved lemon (see page 141), flesh
    removed, rind rinsed and finely chopped
2 eggs, lightly beaten
¼ cup (3 tablespoons) flat-leaf parsley,
    roughly chopped
1½ teaspoons sea salt
freshly ground black pepper
1 quantity Gluten-free Pastry (see page 138)
1 egg, extra, beaten with 1 tablespoon
    pouring cream

1 Preheat fan-forced oven to 180° (200°C). Roast pine nuts for 5–8 minutes or until golden. Remove and cool.

2 Place ¼ cup (60 ml) of the verjuice in each of 2 small saucepans, then add currants to one and dried apples to the other. Heat both pans gently over low heat for a few minutes, then set aside for dried fruit to plump and cool.

3 Heat a splash of olive oil in a small frying pan over low–medium heat, then saute onion and garlic for 10 minutes or until translucent but not coloured. Add ginger and cinnamon and cook for another minute until the spices give off a rich scent; take care not to burn. Remove from heat, stir in honey and leave to cool completely.

4 Put minced pork, pine nuts, cooled onion mixture, soaked currants and apple mixtures, preserved lemon, egg, parsley, salt and pepper in a large bowl and mix thoroughly. Cover and refrigerate until ready to use.

5 Divide pastry into 8 even pieces, then roll out each piece between 2 pieces of greased baking paper to make a 3 mm-thick round. Place one-eighth of the filling on the bottom half of each pastry round. Fold pastry over to encase filling, then fold over edges thickly to seal, trimming off any excess pastry. Brush with egg wash, then place on a baking tray lined with baking paper and refrigerate for 10–15 minutes.

6 Preheat fan-forced oven to 230°C (250°C).

7 Bake pasties for 20–25 minutes or until golden, then serve.

Potato gnocchi with prawns

The idea of putting prawns with gnocchi comes from Alex Herbert, after eating her version at her then Sydney restaurant, Bird Cow Fish. My Barossa-inspired take on it is to make it with yabbies instead, when I can get them – either way, it is a beautiful dish.

750 g Nicola or other waxy potatoes, scrubbed
2 eggs, lightly beaten
2½ teaspoons salt
125 g plain flour
170 g cold unsalted butter, chopped
    into small pieces
40 sage leaves (about 1 bunch)
⅓ cup (80 ml) verjuice (see page 141)
extra virgin olive oil, for cooking
12 raw king prawns or yabbies, peeled
    and cleaned, with tails intact
sea salt and freshly ground black pepper

1 Steam potatoes for 30 minutes or until cooked through but not falling apart. Set aside until just cool enough to handle, then peel. Press hot potatoes through a mouli or potato ricer into a bowl, then add egg and salt. Place flour in a rectangular shape on a bench. Spread potato over flour, then quickly mix with a pastry scraper until it comes together to form a dough. Divide dough into quarters, then shape each quarter into a long 2.5 cm-wide sausage. Cut off 1.5 cm pieces, then gently press the tops with the back of a fork's tines to leave an indentation, which will help the gnocchi to pick up more sauce.

2 Preheat fan-forced oven to 200°C (220°C).

3 Bring salted water to the boil in a large deep frying pan and cook gnocchi in batches until they float to the surface (if just made, this could take as little as 30 seconds). Drain well and transfer to a flat dish.

4 Place 150 g butter and sage leaves in a large flat baking dish (mine is 32 cm × 28 cm × 3 cm), spreading butter and sage evenly. Bake for 5 minutes or until sage begins to cook.

5 Increase oven temperature to 230°C fan-forced (250°C). Transfer poached gnocchi to baking dish with butter and sage, then bake for 5 minutes. Toss the dish to flip the gnocchi or turn each one over with a pair of tongs, then drizzle with ¼ cup (60 ml) verjuice and return to the oven for another 3 minutes.

6 Meanwhile, heat remaining butter and a splash of olive oil in a frying pan over high heat until nut-brown, then reduce heat to medium and gently saute prawns (or yabbies) until pink and just cooked through. Season to taste with salt and pepper and deglaze with remaining verjuice. Transfer prawns (or yabbies) and pan juices to gnocchi and stir gently to combine.

7 Divide gnocchi, sage leaves and butter, and prawns or yabbies among 4 wide bowls, then serve immediately.

Pan-fried saltwater barramundi with caramelised lemon and rocket

Wild barramundi has a great flavour and texture, but you must take care when cooking it as it is a really dense-fleshed fish that needs to be cooked through. The caramelised lemon is a true sweet–sour concoction; adding the fresh ginger and lemon thyme at the last minute really balances its flavour beautifully.

unsalted butter, for cooking
extra virgin olive oil, for cooking
4 × 160 g barramundi fillets,
    skin-on and pin-boned
sea salt and freshly ground black pepper
squeeze of lemon juice
rocket leaves, to serve

CARAMELISED LEMON
½ cup (110 g) caster sugar
3 lemons, 2 cut into 5 mm-thick slices,
    and 1 juiced
2 teaspoons finely grated ginger
1 teaspoon finely chopped lemon thyme

1 For the caramelised lemon, place sugar and 1 cup (250 ml) water in a small saucepan and bring to the boil over medium heat, stirring until sugar dissolves. Increase heat to high and boil rapidly for 5 minutes or until a syrup begins to form. Reduce to lowest heat possible (use a simmer mat, if necessary), then add sliced lemons and juice and cook for another 10–15 minutes or until lemon slices are translucent and still hold their shape, taking care that syrup does not darken in colour and caramelise. Remove from heat, then add ginger and lemon thyme and leave to infuse until required.

2 Heat a knob of butter and splash of olive oil in a frying pan over medium–high heat. Season barramundi fillets with salt and pepper, then place in hot pan, skin-side down, and cook for 4–5 minutes or until skin is crisp. Tip excess butter out of pan and add a little more butter, then carefully flip fish over and cook for another 4–5 minutes or until just cooked through and firm to the touch.

3 Add a squeeze of lemon juice to the fish, then serve pan-fried barramundi topped with caramelised lemons (including a little of the syrup) and rocket leaves to the side.

Steamed yabbies with lemon, purslane, roasted tomato and basil

SERVES 4

This dish celebrates the return of yabbies to our dams after a number of very dry years. The roasted tomato juice marries beautifully with the delicate yabby meat. If you can't get hold of purslane, which is salty and juicy, you can substitute lamb's lettuce (mache), but you may need to add more salt.

24 large live yabbies
zest of 2 lemons, removed in thin strips with
    a vegetable peeler, leaving bitter pith
2 small handfuls purslane, plucked into
    2 cm lengths
2 small handfuls basil leaves, shredded
1½ tablespoons lemon juice
¼ cup (60 ml) extra virgin olive oil
sea salt and freshly ground black pepper

ROASTED TOMATO
540 g roma (plum) tomatoes, thickly sliced
¼ cup (60 ml) extra virgin olive oil
2 pinches caster sugar
sea salt and freshly ground black pepper

1 For the roasted tomato, preheat fan-forced oven to 220°C (240°C). Spread tomato slices on baking trays. Brush with olive oil, then sprinkle with caster sugar and season with salt and pepper. Roast for 40 minutes or until evenly cooked.

2 Meanwhile, stun yabbies in freezer in a tightly covered container for 20 minutes. Bring a large stockpot of water to the boil and place a steamer on top. Working in batches, put a few yabbies and some zest in steamer, then cover tightly. Rapidly return to the boil and steam for 4–6 minutes. Reserve 4 whole yabbies and lemon zest. Peel remaining yabbies and remove intestinal tracts.

3 Mix peeled yabbies in a large bowl with purslane, basil, reserved lemon zest and roasted tomato. Whisk lemon juice and olive oil together and season with salt and pepper, then toss through salad. Divide among plates or serve on a large platter, with whole yabbies perched on top.

Salmon poached in olive oil with tomato and avocado salsa   SERVES 4

This is a very special, even sensuous dish. It works best when the salmon fillets are the same size and weight (ideally from the centre of the fish). The cooked salmon is quite pink inside and warm rather than hot, so make sure your guests don't belong to the 'if it's not piping hot, it's not right' school of thought!

4 salmon fillets, skin removed
   and pin-boned
extra virgin olive oil
sea salt

TOMATO AND AVOCADO SALSA
4 small ripe tomatoes, seeded and
   cut into 5 mm dice
1 very small red onion, cut into 5 mm dice
½ large Reed avocado, cut into 5 mm dice
6 basil leaves, torn
1 cup (250 ml) mellow extra virgin olive oil
juice of 1 lemon
sea salt and freshly ground black pepper

1 For the salsa, just before serving, gently combine tomato, onion, avocado and basil with olive oil and lemon juice, then season with salt and pepper and set aside at room temperature for flavours to meld.

2 Choose a heavy-based saucepan or deep frying pan large enough to fit the fish – the smaller the pan, the less olive oil you will need to use. Pour a generous amount of olive oil into the pan, then heat over very low heat and bring to blood temperature only (dip your finger into the oil – it should not feel hot). Slip fillets into oil – they should lay just below the surface like submarines – and cook for 18–22 minutes. If white dots appear on the surface of the fish, the oil is too hot (these are beads of protein), so reduce the temperature.

3 Remove salmon from pan with an egg slice and put straight onto waiting plates.

4 Mound some salsa, including the dressing, on top of each fillet, and serve immediately with sea salt on the table. (The salmon will be quite pink in the centre but will be cooked.)

Snapper in a parcel

Serving fish en papillote is a breeze, and it means that you can create any number of different sauces by adding a few flavourings to the parcel before cooking: a little butter, cream, extra virgin olive oil, wine, fresh herbs, slices of Meyer lemon or a dash of lemon or lime juice, in whatever combination takes your fancy. Salmon fillets or cutlets are also delicious when treated this way.

extra virgin olive oil, for cooking
1 small bulb fennel, trimmed and sliced,
    fronds reserved
4 × 200 g snapper fillets of equal thickness,
    skin removed and pin-boned
1 Meyer lemon, sliced
handful fresh chervil sprigs or
    bay leaves (optional)
sea salt and freshly ground black pepper
boiled waxy potatoes, green vegetables
    or salad (optional), to serve

1 Heat a little olive oil in a frying pan, then saute fennel over medium heat until cooked through.

2 Preheat fan-forced oven to 200°C (220°C).

3 Liberally oil 4 sheets of baking paper or foil large enough to wrap each fish fillet. Arrange cooked fennel and reserved fronds on each one as a bed for the fish. Position fillets on top, then add lemon slices and chervil or bay leaves, if using. Drizzle with olive oil, then season with salt and pepper and carefully fold in the edges to seal each parcel. Transfer parcels to a baking tray (a scone tray is ideal for this) and bake for 8 minutes. Leave fish to rest for another 5 minutes before serving.

4 When everyone opens their parcels they will be surrounded by a wonderful aroma as the juices spill onto the plate. Drizzle over a little more olive oil, add a boiled waxy spud and a green vegie or salad, if desired, and your meal is complete.

Macaroni cheese

My mother often made this rich and luscious dish when relatives came to dinner. Mum never wrote down a recipe in her life, so I only have the memory of what she did to go by. I've added my own touch by introducing roasted pumpkin and Persian feta.

1.2 kg Kent or Queensland blue pumpkin,
  peeled, seeded and cut into small chunks
4 stalks rosemary, leaves picked and chopped
sea salt
extra virgin olive oil, for cooking
¼ cup (60 ml) verjuice (see page 141)
2 litres milk
2 fresh bay leaves
160 g unsalted butter, chopped
160 g plain flour
1 tablespoon freshly grated or ground nutmeg
250 g grated Parmigiano Reggiano
400 g large macaroni
150 g Persian goat's feta, crumbled
250 g grated cheddar

1 Preheat fan-forced oven to 200°C (220°C).

2 Line a baking tray with baking paper, then add pumpkin and rosemary, season generously with salt and drizzle with olive oil. Roast for 30 minutes or until pumpkin is tender and starting to brown. Drizzle verjuice over pumpkin, then bake until verjuice has evaporated.

3 Meanwhile, heat milk with bay leaves in a saucepan over high heat until almost boiling, then remove from heat and leave to infuse for 10 minutes. Remove and discard bay leaves and keep milk hot.

4 Melt butter in a saucepan over medium heat until nut-brown. Add flour and cook until flour and butter come together, stirring for several minutes. Remove from heat and slowly pour in hot milk, whisking to incorporate and prevent lumps forming. Return to heat and stir with a wooden spoon for another 10 minutes or until sauce is shiny and coats back of spoon. Add nutmeg and Parmigiano, stirring until cheese has melted. (Only season with salt after adding the Parmigiano as it can be salty enough.) Cover surface of sauce closely with plastic film to stop a skin forming and set aside.

5 Cook macaroni in a large saucepan of boiling salted water until al dente, then drain and place in a bowl. Add cheese sauce and mix through well, then add pumpkin and gently toss. Gently stir in feta. Transfer mixture to a 2.5 litre-capacity baking dish (mine is a 40 cm × 30 cm × 5 cm), top with cheddar and bake for 10–20 minutes or until brown. Serve.

Pumpkin risotto

If you can't find pumpkin with ripe, deep ochre-coloured flesh, then don't bother to make this. Buying pre-cut pumpkin is preferable as you can see what you are getting. Whilst Queensland Blue was the pumpkin of my childhood, Kent pumpkins are more readily available and usually of good quality. And don't forget butternut pumpkin, which is a little more forgiving as it's naturally sweeter.

1 kg ripe pumpkin, peeled, seeded and cut into 2 cm chunks
⅓ cup (80 ml) extra virgin olive oil, plus extra for drizzling
80 g unsalted butter, chopped
1 onion, finely chopped
1–1.25 litres Vegetable Stock (see page 132) or Golden Chicken Stock (see page 132)
2 cups (400 g) risotto rice
½ cup (125 ml) verjuice (see page 141)
1½ teaspoons sea salt
100 g freshly grated Parmigiano Reggiano, plus extra shaved, to serve
chopped flat-leaf parsley, to serve

1 Preheat fan-forced oven to 210°C (230°C).

2 Toss pumpkin with half of the olive oil in a bowl to coat, then spread on a baking tray lined with baking paper and roast for 20–25 minutes or until cooked and coloured but still firm.

3 Meanwhile, melt butter with remaining olive oil in a heavy-based saucepan over medium heat, then add onion and saute for 10 minutes or until light golden.

4 Bring stock to the boil in a saucepan over high heat and keep warm.

5 Add rice to pan with onion and stir to coat, then increase heat to high. Make a well in centre of rice, then add verjuice and cook, stirring, until verjuice has evaporated. Stir in salt. Reduce heat to medium and add hot stock to rice mixture, a ladleful at a time, stirring continuously and waiting for each addition to be absorbed before adding the next.

6 When you have used half the stock, add half the roasted pumpkin, using a spoon to mash pumpkin into rice a little. Add remaining stock as above and continue to cook until rice is al dente and mixture is thick and syrupy: the whole cooking time should be about 20 minutes. Stir through Parmigiano and check for seasoning.

7 Spoon risotto into serving dishes and top with remaining roasted pumpkin and chopped parsley. Drizzle with olive oil and serve with shaved Parmigiano offered at the table.

End

I love the idea of setting fruit in a tart filling. Here, poached quince cuts through the richness of the chocolate and gives the tart a luscious deep colour when cut.

750 g quinces, peeled, cored and cut into large wedges, cores and skin reserved
squeeze of lemon juice
200 ml verjuice (see page 141), plus 100 ml extra, as needed
¾ cup (165 g) caster sugar
½ quantity Sour-cream Pastry (see page 138)
Dutch-process cocoa powder, for dusting
whipped cream, to serve

CHOCOLATE ALMOND CREAM

120 g unsalted butter, softened
150 g caster sugar
2 eggs
1 egg yolk
50 g dark Dutch-process cocoa powder
⅓ cup (80 ml) vino cotto (see page 141)
200 g ground almonds

1 Preheat fan-forced oven to 170°C (190°C).

2 Place quince wedges in a bowl of cold water with a squeeze of lemon to prevent them discolouring. Wrap and tie quince cores and skin in a piece of muslin, then place in a heavy-based ovenproof saucepan or enamelled cast-iron casserole with the verjuice, sugar and 300 ml water. Bring to the boil over high heat to dissolve sugar and begin making a syrup. Add drained quince and bring back to the boil, then top with a piece of baking paper cut to fit the surface (cartouche). Cover with a tight-fitting lid.

3 Transfer to the oven and roast quince for 1 hour, then gently turn quince over, taking care not to break up the wedges. Return to oven and cook for another 2 hours or until quince is tender and deep ruby-red but still maintaining its shape, checking every 30 minutes to make sure the liquid

has not evaporated; add extra verjuice if necessary to prevent the quince from catching. (The liquid should reduce to a small amount of syrup in base of pan.) Remove quince from pan and place on a wire rack or paper-towel-lined plate to drain excess syrup. Set aside to cool.

4 Increase oven temperature to 200°C fan-forced (220°C).

5 For the chocolate almond cream, place butter and sugar in an electric mixer, then process for 6 minutes or until light and creamy. Add eggs and yolk, one at a time and mixing after adding each one, then add cocoa and vino cotto and mix for a further 1 minute. Add ground almonds and mix until well combined. Set aside.

6 Grease a 24 cm tart tin with a removable base. Roll out pastry on a lightly floured bench until 2–3 mm thick, then use to line tart tin. Cut off excess pastry around edge, leaving 5 mm to allow for shrinkage as it cooks. Refrigerate for 20 minutes.

7 Prick pastry base with a fork, then line with foil, fill with pastry weights and blind bake for 15 minutes. Remove foil and weights and bake for a further 5 minutes or until pastry looks dry. Remove from oven and leave for 10–15 minutes or until cool.

8 Reduce oven temperature to 175°C fan-forced (195°C). Spread one-third of the chocolate almond cream over base of tart shell, then top with quince. Dot remaining chocolate almond cream over quince.

9 Bake the tart for 50 minutes–1 hour or until chocolate almond cream is cooked in the centre and the surface of the tart is golden (if the surface is browning too quickly, reduce oven temperature to 165°C fan-forced [185°C] and continue baking until the centre is cooked through).

10 Leave tart to cool completely in tin. Dust with cocoa, then slice and serve with whipped cream.

Rhubarb crumble

As I love rhubarb I have eight large 'crowns' of a deep ruby-red variety growing in my garden. I came across a grower at the local Saturday Barossa Farmers' Market who grows a pale-green variety, which, he says, is a little sweeter than my more traditional variety. I found this quite fascinating as I don't like to add a lot of sugar when cooking rhubarb, so I'd be really happy to have a variety on hand that requires even less sugar than I use now.

1 large bunch (about 1 kg) ripe rhubarb, leaves discarded and stems washed and cut into 4 cm pieces (discard any brown bits)
½ cup (110 g) caster sugar or ¼ cup (90 g) honey
finely grated zest and juice of 2 oranges, plus extra juice as needed
125 g plain flour
1 teaspoon ground cinnamon
⅓ cup (75 g) dark brown sugar
100 g rolled oats
140 g chilled unsalted butter, chopped
double cream, to serve

1 Preheat fan-forced oven to 180°C (200°C).

2 Spread rhubarb in a baking dish, sprinkle with caster sugar or honey and orange juice and bake for 20 minutes or until tender, then set rhubarb and pan juices aside. Add a little extra orange juice if there are no juices left in the dish.

3 Combine flour, cinnamon, sugar, orange zest and oats, then rub butter into flour using your fingertips.

4 Place rhubarb and pan juices in a buttered 1 litre-capacity baking dish or four 1 cup (250 ml) ramekins, sprinkle with crumble, then bake for 15 minutes (for ramekins) or 25 minutes (if baking in one dish) or until golden.

5 Serve crumble with double cream offered alongside.

Dianne's scones with mulberry and verjuice jam

Dianne Wooldridge is our master sconemaker at the Farmshop. In four years of filming *The Cook and the Chef*, she helped a great deal in many ways, but I think it was the morning-tea scones she whipped up without a second thought that endeared her most to the crew. I have to say she doesn't even weigh anything, but just throws the ingredients together, so we had to watch her very carefully to get this recipe right. Chris Wotton, my product development chef, picked the mulberries to make the jam. Our mulberry tree is of the old-fashioned variety that makes your hands purple as you pick the berries, but who cares when the flavour of the darkest, ripest ones is so special that it's hard not to just keep on eating as you're picking? This makes a small amount of jam and it's very quick to make: great for when guests pop around at short notice. It doesn't set firm like regular jam, but rather is a nice syrupy consistency – perfect for dolloping onto scones.

4 cups (600 g) plain flour, plus
    extra for dusting
1½ tablespoons baking powder
pinch of salt
⅓ cup (55 g) icing sugar
2 cups (500 ml) thickened cream
⅔ cup (160 ml) milk
whipped cream, to serve

MULBERRY AND VERJUICE JAM
300 g mulberries
100 ml verjuice (see page 141)
125 g caster sugar
1 tablespoon lemon juice

1 To make the jam, place the mulberries, verjuice and caster sugar in a saucepan over high heat, then bring to the boil and boil rapidly for 5 minutes. Add the lemon juice and boil for a further 5 minutes or until the jam is a syrupy consistency. Leave to cool for 15 minutes, then pour into a warm sterilised jar and seal.

2 Preheat a fan-forced oven to 180°C (200°C) and line a baking tray with baking paper.

3 Sift together the flour, baking powder, salt and icing sugar into a large bowl. Make a well in the centre and gradually fold in the cream and the milk until you have a soft dough (it shouldn't be sloppy or dry – you may need to use more or less cream and milk, depending on the moisture content of the flour). Take care not to over-mix.

4 Turn out the dough onto a lightly floured bench and gently pat down to flatten it out to a thickness of 3 cm. Use a 5 cm round cutter to cut out 24 discs and place them close together on the prepared baking tray. Bake for 20–25 minutes or until golden and well risen.

5 Serve the scones with a bowl of mulberry and verjuice jam and some whipped cream to the side.

Cherry clafoutis

The dark, very juicy cherry varieties are my favourites and are a perfect foil to a clafoutis batter. I leave the stones in the cherries as you lose juice when you remove them. I tend to serve this in early summer before the weather heats up as it's best eaten warm from the oven with a good dollop of thick cream. The recipe can be halved, if preferred.

20 g unsalted butter
300 g caster sugar
1⅓ cups (200 g) unbleached plain flour
½ teaspoon baking powder
1 pinch salt
300 ml milk
300 ml pouring cream
6 eggs
1 teaspoon pure vanilla extract
400 g cherries, washed, stalks removed
icing sugar, for dusting

1 Preheat fan-forced oven to 200°C (220°C).

2 Melt butter, then brush a shallow 1.2 litre-capacity ceramic or glass baking dish with this and sprinkle over 1 tablespoon of the caster sugar to coat evenly.

3 Sift flour, baking powder and salt into an electric mixer, then add remaining caster sugar. Whisk milk, cream, eggs and vanilla extract in another bowl, then, with mixer running at medium speed, slowly pour milk mixture into flour to make a smooth batter.

4 Arrange cherries over base of prepared dish and pour over batter. Bake for 20–30 minutes until golden and set. Dust with icing sugar and serve immediately.

Orchard cake

This is based on a recipe I was given for a Jewish cake which I have adapted by using different types and ratios of fruit. What makes it so special is that nearly all the ingredients I use – everything except the butter, sugar and spices – come from my own orchard. What a joy it is to be able to use your own produce. This cake can be made with purchased dried fruit; just ensure it is of top-notch quality. Remember – bitter almonds are poisonous if eaten to excess.

90 g dried figs
90 g dried nectarines
90 g dried apricots
90 g dried peaches
1¼ cups (310 ml) verjuice (see page 141)
180 g dried currants
60 g blanched almonds
120 g dark-brown sugar
180 g unsalted butter, chopped
4 eggs
180 g self-raising flour
½ teaspoon ground cinnamon
½ teaspoon ground nutmeg
120 g candied lemon peel or mixed peel
finely grated zest of 1 lemon
candied orange rind (optional), to serve

ALMOND PASTE

1¼ cups (120 g) blanched almonds
2 bitter almonds
100 g icing sugar
1 egg yolk

1 Place figs, nectarines, apricots and peaches in a bowl with 1 cup (250 ml) verjuice and soak for at least 1 hour. Strain fruit, reserving verjuice, then cut into pieces. Soak currants in reserved verjuice for 30 minutes or more, then drain, again reserving verjuice.

2 Preheat fan-forced oven to 220°C (240°C). Grease and line a deep 20 cm round cake tin with baking paper.

3 Put the 60 g almonds for the cake onto a baking tray and the 120 g almonds and 2 bitter almonds for almond paste on a separate baking tray, then dry-roast for 6–8 minutes. Set aside to cool separately. Reduce oven temperature to fan-forced 180°C (200°C).

4 For the almond paste, blend cooled almonds and bitter almonds in a food processor, then add icing sugar and egg yolk and pulse to form a stiff paste. Set aside.

5 Using hand-held electric beaters, cream brown sugar and butter until pale and fluffy. Beat in one egg at a time, adding a spoonful of flour if mixture curdles. Fold in flour, spices, drained fruit, almonds and candied peel. Stir lemon zest and remaining verjuice into mixture to give a soft batter. Spoon half the batter into prepared tin, then spread almond paste over and top with remaining batter.

6 Bake for 2½ hours or until a fine skewer inserted into centre of cake comes out clean. Leave cake to cool a little in the tin before turning out to cool completely on a wire rack. Serve, topped with candied orange rind, if desired.

I absolutely love blood oranges: I never tire of freshly squeezed blood orange juice for breakfast or added to a glass of Campari later in the day. I make more blood orange confit than is needed here as I enjoy serving it as a sweetmeat with a cup of strong espresso or sometimes I even dip them into melted chocolate for an after-dinner treat.

½ quantity Sour-cream Pastry (see page 138)

CHOCOLATE GANACHE
1 cup (250 ml) double cream
250 g dark couverture chocolate
(70 per cent cocoa solids),
finely chopped
10 g unsalted butter

BLOOD ORANGE CONFIT
⅓ cup (75 g) caster sugar
2 blood oranges, thinly sliced
juice of 1 lemon

1 For the blood orange confit, bring sugar and ⅓ cup (80 ml) water slowly to the boil over low heat, stirring constantly until sugar dissolves. Leave to cool.

2 Preheat fan-forced oven to 150°C (170°C).

3 Lay orange slices in a baking dish so they overlap slightly. Pour over cooled syrup and cover with baking paper and foil. Bake orange slices for 1 hour, then remove foil and baking paper and return to the oven to cook until the syrup is thick and orange slices are caramelised; this can take another 30–60 minutes. Squeeze lemon juice over to give the syrup a glossy sheen. Store in an airtight container in the refrigerator for up to 1 month.

4 Preheat fan-forced oven to 220°C (240°C).

5 Roll out pastry on a lightly floured bench, then gently place over a 22 cm tart tin with a removable base, pressing pastry into side of tin and leaving an overhanging border. Line pastry with foil, fill with pastry weights or dried beans and blind bake for 12 minutes, then trim pastry to edges of the tin. Remove foil and weights and bake for another 5 minutes or until pale-golden and dry. Leave tart shell in the tin on a wire rack to cool.

6 For the chocolate ganache, bring cream to the boil in a heavy-based saucepan over medium heat. Place chocolate in a heatproof bowl and pour boiling cream over. Set aside for 3 minutes, then stir to melt chocolate. Add butter to warm chocolate mixture to give ganache a shiny finish. Pour ganache into cooled tart shell and refrigerate for 1 hour or until set.

7 Place slices of blood orange confit in the centre of tart then cut into slices and serve.

Sultana cake

This cake takes inspiration from a recipe in the book *Riches from the Vine*, produced in 1994 by a local women's group, the Soroptimist International of Barossa Valley Inc. Given my inclination for generous flavours, I've added more grapes, more lemon – well, basically more of everything. The outcome is a cake that is so incredibly moist it lasts for days – that is, if anyone has the strength of character to not keep going back for more.

3 × 55 g eggs
150 g caster sugar
⅓ cup (80 ml) extra virgin olive oil
60 g unsalted butter, melted
75 ml milk
1⅓ cups (200 g) plain flour
1 teaspoon baking powder
finely grated zest of 4 lemons
large pinch freshly grated or
    ground nutmeg
500 g fresh seedless green grapes
    (about 3 cups picked grapes)
1 tablespoon demerara sugar
icing sugar (optional), for dusting

1 Preheat fan-forced oven to 180°C (200°C). Grease and line a deep 20 cm springform cake tin with baking paper.

2 Using hand-held electric beaters, beat eggs and caster sugar until pale and thick. Add olive oil, butter and milk and mix well.

3 In a separate bowl, sift together flour and baking powder, then stir in lemon zest and nutmeg. Tip flour mixture into egg mixture and fold to combine. Add two-thirds of the picked grapes and gently stir to just combine, then pour into prepared cake tin.

4 Bake cake for 15 minutes. Remove from oven and sprinkle with remaining grapes and demerara sugar. Bake for another 40 minutes or until a skewer inserted into the centre of the cake comes out clean. Allow cake to cool in tin for a few minutes, then turn cake out onto a wire rack and leave to cool.

5 Dust cooled cake with icing sugar, if using, then cut into slices and serve.

Olive oil dessert cake with poached loquats

Whilst Alice Waters' famous olive oil and sauternes cake was the initial inspiration for this, further research showed that olive oil has long been added to Italian cakes to give an incredibly moist finish. Loquats are so often ignored. Hating waste, I added their syrup to this cake: you could use the same quantity of dessert wine instead.

5 large egg yolks
finely grated zest of 5 lemons
145 g caster sugar
½ cup (125 ml) syrup from the
    poached loquats (see below)
½ cup (125 ml) extra virgin olive oil
1 cup (150 g) unbleached plain flour
pinch of salt
3 egg whites
pinch of cream of tartar
icing sugar, for dusting

POACHED LOQUATS
280 g caster sugar
400 ml white wine
2 vanilla beans, split lengthways
zest of 3 lemons, removed in strips
    with a vegetable peeler,
    leaving bitter pith
12 loquats, peeled carefully
⅔ cup (160 ml) lemon juice

1 For the poached loquats, bring caster sugar and ¼ cup (60 ml) water to the boil in a saucepan over medium heat and cook until amber-coloured. Carefully add wine, vanilla beans and lemon zest, taking care as the mixture will spit. Bring to a gentle simmer, then add loquats and poach for about 10 minutes or until just tender. (The timing will depend upon the ripeness of the loquats.) Add a little of the lemon juice to the syrup at a time to reduce the sweetness, tasting as you go. Measure and reserve ½ cup (125 ml) of the syrup. Set loquats and remaining syrup aside.

2 Preheat fan-forced oven to 180°C (200°C). Grease and line a 22 cm springform cake tin.

3 Beat egg yolks with lemon zest and half the caster sugar in an electric mixer until thick and pale. With the mixer on low speed, slowly add reserved poaching syrup, then olive oil. Sift flour and salt over mixture and beat until smooth.

4 In a clean bowl, beat egg whites with cream of tartar until soft peaks form. Slowly add remaining caster sugar and continue to beat to make a thick, soft meringue. Fold a spoonful of meringue into batter. Pour batter into meringue and fold until well incorporated.

5 Spoon batter into prepared tin and bake for 20 minutes. Reduce oven temperature to 160°C fan-forced (180°C) and bake for a further 20 minutes or until a fine skewer inserted in the centre comes out clean. Remove cake from oven and place a buttered round of baking paper on top to stop cake from drying out, then leave to cool.

6 Remove cake from the tin, dust with icing sugar and serve with loquats and their syrup.

Fig and Walnut Tart

I made this tart so often at the Pheasant Farm that I became tired of it, and was almost embarrassed by the enthusiastic response as it couldn't be more simple. Twenty years later, I now enjoy making it again, having replaced the original cream with crème fraîche. Last time I made it, I topped the tart with slices of fresh lime and was transported. A recipe is only a base, after all.

180 g walnuts
330 g dried figs
6 free-range egg whites
250 g soft dark-brown sugar
crème fraîche
slices of candied *or* fresh lime (optional)

1 Preheat the oven to 220°C. Roast the walnuts on a baking tray for about 5 minutes, shaking the trays to prevent the nuts from burning. If they are not fresh season's, rub the walnuts in a clean tea towel to remove the bitter skins, then sieve away the skins. Allow to cool. Reduce the oven temperature to 180°C.

2 Line and grease a 24 cm springform cake tin. Remove the hard stem from each fig, then chop the figs into small pieces (this should give you 1½ cups). Toss the walnuts and fig pieces together.

3 In the bowl of an electric mixer, whisk the egg whites to soft peaks, then slowly add the soft dark-brown sugar in heaped tablespoons until incorporated and the resultant meringue is thick and stiff. Take a spoonful of the meringue and mix it through the figs and walnuts. Tip this back into the meringue and fold it through. Spoon the meringue mixture into the prepared cake tin and bake for 45–50 minutes; until the tart pulls away from the sides and feels 'set' on top.

4 Allow to cool and serve with a good dollop of crème fraîche. Candied or even fresh lime is a wonderful accompaniment to this tart – decorate the edge of the tart with a ring of fine, fine slices of the lime. The tart is meant to be sticky and soft and will be rustic in appearance, so don't fret if it falls apart as you serve it.

Baked peaches with almond and ginger butter

Ripe peaches bring to mind that wonderful burden of having an abundance of fruit – when the whole tree ripens at once, the spoils must be shared. I've always believed in this philosophy, never more so than now that we have bought our neighbour's stone-fruit orchard. Watch this space as I deal with the true meaning of abundance when the fruit from these 2000 trees ripens.

120 g glace ginger
200 g blanched almonds, roughly chopped
100 g caster sugar
200 g unsalted butter, chopped
10 peaches, cut in half and pitted

1 Mix ginger, almonds and caster sugar together in a small bowl, then rub in the butter and chill in the refrigerator for 20 minutes.

2 Preheat fan-forced oven to 200°C (220°C).

3 Hollow out peaches slightly to make a bigger hole, and bake for 10 minutes, then leave to cool slightly. Add a large dollop of almond mixture to each and bake for a further 10 minutes. Serve.

Cold lemon souffle

We made this simple dessert at the Pheasant Farm in large quantities, and served scoops as it was ordered, sometimes topped with candied strips of lemon zest (see photo opposite). We once had a similar dessert when eating with friends in France's Dordogne region, where a large communal bowl was brought to the table for us to help ourselves. This gesture showed such flair and generosity, and while no one kept tabs on us, none of us abused the privilege.

3 × 61 g eggs, separated
finely grated zest and juice of 3 lemons
  (you need 100 ml strained juice)
100 g caster sugar
2 × 2 g gelatine leaves
¼ cup (60 ml) hot water
300 ml rich double cream (45% fat)

1 Bring a large saucepan of water to the boil. Place egg yolks, zest, juice and caster sugar in a large stainless-steel bowl and set this over the boiling water, then whisk until pale and thick. Remove the bowl and set it aside.

2 Soften gelatine in a little cold water for 5 minutes, then squeeze out any excess moisture and dissolve gelatine in the hot water. Whisk into the egg mixture and refrigerate until cold and just starting to set. Whisk cream until soft peaks form, then fold this through the cold egg-yolk mixture. Refrigerate until just starting to set.

3 Whisk egg whites until soft peaks form (be careful not to overwhip or the final dessert will be crumbly rather than soft and light) and fold these through too. Spoon mixture into individual glasses or dishes or a large bowl and refrigerate until set, about 3 hours. Serve.

Dessert is my least favourite part of the meal, but this dish, passed on to me by Hazel Mader, the mother of my friend Jenny Beckmann, is one of such simplicity it's a favourite of mine when quince is in season. The effect of the long cooking is that the quinces change from bright yellow to a deep ruby-red. They remain whole, but are so well cooked you can even eat the cores! This recipe works for small–medium quinces that will not fall apart when cooked for a long time. Avoid super-large or pineapple variety quinces for this dish.

**6 small–medium quinces, picked with stems
    and leaves intact if possible**
4 cups (880 g) caster sugar
juice of 3 lemons
**cream or Creme Anglaise (optional,
    see page 139), to serve**

1 Rub the down off the quinces and wash them. Pack them tightly in a heavy-based saucepan with the sugar and 1.5 litres water. Boil at a reasonably high temperature until a jelly starts to form, then reduce heat to low and simmer for up to 5 hours (I often use a simmer mat to control the temperature). The quinces should be turned at least 4 times during the cooking process so that the deep-ruby colour goes right through to the core. Add lemon juice at the last stage of cooking to remove excessive sweetness.

2 Serve quinces whole or sliced with a little of the jelly and cream or creme anglaise alongside.

Apricot and almond tart

Dried Australian apricots are the reason for this luscious tart's existence. I've always felt strongly about supporting Australian apricot growers: not only are you keeping a tradition alive, you are buying fruit of intensely superior flavour. We recently bought our neighbour's stone-fruit orchard to save the 2000 mostly apricot, but some peach, nectarine and plum trees from being pulled out, so this is our first year of being stone-fruit growers in addition to our other farming pursuits. Already we've discovered that growing apricots for drying is like buying a lottery ticket but missing the jackpot most of the time.

200 g Australian dried apricots
¾ cup (180 ml) verjuice (see page 141)
120 g unsalted butter
150 g caster sugar
2 eggs
2 tablespoons brandy
finely grated zest of ½ lemon
2 tablespoons plain flour, plus extra
**   for dusting**
200 g ground almonds
½ quantity Sour-cream Pastry (see page 138)
pouring cream, to serve

1 Soak apricots in verjuice overnight or for at least several hours. (Alternatively, microwave apricots and verjuice on low for 2 minutes, then set aside for 20 minutes to reconstitute.)

2 Using an electric mixer, beat the butter and sugar together until pale and creamy. Add one egg at a time, beating a little after adding each one to ensure mixture doesn't curdle. Add brandy and lemon zest and mix to combine, then add flour and ground almonds. Mix to combine well and set aside. Drain apricots and reserve any remaining verjuice.

3 Grease a 22 cm × 4.5 cm-deep tart tin with a removable base. Roll out pastry on a lightly floured bench until 2–3 mm thick, then use to line tart tin. Cut off excess pastry around edge, leaving 5 mm to allow for shrinkage as it cooks. Refrigerate for 20 minutes.

4 Preheat a fan-forced oven to 200°C (220°C).

5 Prick pastry base with a fork, then line with foil, fill with pastry weights and blind bake for 15 minutes. Remove foil and weights and bake for a further 5 minutes or until pastry looks dry. Leave for 10–15 minutes until cool.

6 Reduce oven temperature to 175°C fan-forced (195°C). Spread almond mixture in tart shell, then top with apricots, cut-side up, and brush surface with any reserved verjuice. Bake tart for 30–40 minutes or until a toothpick inserted in centre of almond mixture comes out clean.

7 Serve warm or at room temperature with a jug of cream alongside.

Christmas pudding with brandy butter

My Christmas pudding is so heavy with Barossa dried fruit that it needs no sugar at all. Rather than suet, which I love but which makes this pudding far too dense, I use butter, which means leftovers make the moistest cake imaginable. The brandy butter is based on a recipe from my former editor's mother – the cumquat brandy is my touch.

115 g candied cumquats, chopped
250 g mixed peel
225 g currants
225 g seedless raisins
225 g sultanas
75 g flaked almonds
300 ml Amontillado sherry
115 g unbleached plain flour, plus
    extra for dusting
good pinch of ground cinnamon
good pinch of freshly grated nutmeg
good pinch of ground ginger
good pinch of ground mace
teaspoon salt
225 g chilled unsalted butter
225 g fresh breadcrumbs
3 eggs

BRANDY BUTTER
175 g icing sugar
175 g unsalted butter, softened
½ cup (125 ml) cumquat brandy or
    ⅔ cup (160 ml) brandy

1 Combine cumquat, mixed peel, dried fruit, almonds and sherry in a large stainless-steel or glass bowl and mix thoroughly. Cover with plastic film and leave at room temperature for 24 hours, stirring several times.

2 Sift flour, spices and salt into a large bowl, then grate in butter coarsely. Stir in breadcrumbs and add fruit mixture. Whisk eggs until light and frothy and stir through pudding mixture until well combined.

3 Dust a 30 cm square of calico with a little flour, then spoon pudding mixture into the centre. Gather up the cloth and tie it securely with string at top of pudding. Steam the pudding in a large double steamer or boil in a large saucepan for 6 hours, replenishing the water every 30 minutes or as necessary. Suspend boiled pudding in a cool, airy place to mature before using – I make ours in October. (Puddings can become mouldy if the weather is humid or if several are hung too close together, so if you don't have time to mature your pudding, or the weather is against you, it won't matter.)

4 Make the brandy butter on Christmas morning (it can be made the day before but it needs to be wrapped really well to avoid it becoming tainted in the refrigerator). Cream icing sugar and butter in an electric mixer until white, thick and fluffy and sugar has dissolved. (This takes some time, so be patient.) Slowly beat in brandy, a teaspoonful at a time, tasting as you go (you may not need it all). Cover with plastic film and refrigerate.

5 To serve, steam pudding in its cloth in the top of a steamer or double saucepan for 1 hour or until heated through. Meanwhile, let brandy butter stand at room temperature for 20 minutes, then transfer it to 2 serving bowls so people can help themselves.

Basics

Golden chicken stock

There is something very satisfying about making your own stock. I use verjuice rather than white wine when deglazing the bones, which gives a gentle acidity to the stock: otherwise I find it can be a little 'flat'.

1 × 2.2 kg boiling chicken, cut into pieces
    (or 3 kg chicken bones)
2 large onions, halved
1 large carrot, roughly chopped
extra virgin olive oil, for cooking
100 ml verjuice (see page 141)
1 large leek, white part only, trimmed,
    washed and roughly chopped
1 stick celery, roughly chopped
1 fresh bay leaf
6 sprigs thyme
6 stalks flat-leaf parsley
1 head garlic, halved widthways

1 Preheat fan-forced oven to 200°C (220°C).

2 Place chicken, onion and carrot in a roasting pan and drizzle with a little olive oil. Roast for 20–25 minutes or until golden brown.

3 Transfer chicken and vegetables to a large stockpot and place roasting pan on stove over high heat. Add verjuice and simmer for 30 seconds or so, stirring and scraping bottom of pan, then tip pan juices into stockpot. Add leek, celery, bay leaf, thyme, parsley, garlic and about 4 litres water to stockpot; the chicken and vegetables should be covered. Bring to simmering point, then simmer uncovered for 3 hours.

4 Strain stock immediately through a fine-mesh sieve into a bowl, then cool quickly by placing bowl in a sink of cold water. Refrigerate or freeze until needed, removing any solidified fat from surface before using. This stock will keep for up to 4 days in the refrigerator or 3 months in the freezer.

Vegetable stock

This is a great all-purpose stock that can be used in all kinds of soups, risottos and braises. You can vary the vegetables depending on what you have to hand.

2 tablespoons extra virgin olive oil
1 large onion, quartered
1 clove garlic, roughly chopped
2 carrots, roughly chopped
2 sticks celery, roughly chopped
1 leek, white part only, trimmed,
    washed and roughly chopped
1½ tablespoons verjuice (see page 141)
50 g mushrooms, quartered
1 potato, roughly chopped
2 stalks flat-leaf parsley
1 sprig thyme

1 Heat olive oil in a large stockpot over medium heat, then add onion and cook for 8 minutes until golden brown. Add garlic, carrot, celery and leek and cook for a further 4 minutes. Increase heat to high and add verjuice, stirring until it evaporates. Add remaining ingredients and 2 litres water, then bring to the boil. Reduce heat to low and simmer gently for 2 hours or until stock has reduced by a third.

2 Strain stock immediately through a fine-mesh sieve into a bowl and set aside to cool, then refrigerate or freeze until needed. This stock will keep for up to 4 days in the refrigerator or 3 months in the freezer.

I tend to make a big pot of this stock, then freeze leftovers to have on hand to create that soup, risotto or last-minute sauce where using a good fish stock will make all the difference.

1 kg snapper heads
20 g unsalted butter
½ large onion, diced
½ leek, white part only, trimmed,
  washed and roughly chopped
½ carrot, diced
½ stick celery, diced
2 button mushrooms, sliced
1 cup (250 ml) verjuice (see page 141)
6 stalks flat-leaf parsley
2 sprigs thyme
1 bay leaf
6 black peppercorns

1 To clean snapper heads, cut around pointed underside of head and gills, then pull away whole bottom part of heads and discard. Scrape out any traces of blood or innards, then rinse heads carefully.

2 Melt butter in a large stainless-steel stockpot over low–medium heat, then add onion, leek, carrot, celery and mushroom and cook for 2 minutes, stirring occasionally to make sure they don't brown. Add fish heads and cook for 1 minute. Increase heat to high and pour in verjuice. Bring to the boil and boil vigorously for 2 minutes. Pour in 2 litres water, then add parsley, thyme, bay leaf and peppercorns. Bring to simmering point, then reduce heat to low and simmer for 20 minutes (don't allow the stock to boil at this stage as it will become cloudy).

3 Strain stock immediately through a fine-mesh sieve into a bowl and set aside to cool. This stock will keep for up to 4 days in the refrigerator or 3 months in the freezer.

Bechamel sauce

Bechamel sauce was only ever known as white sauce when I was growing up. I learnt to make it at a very young age, judiciously adding the milk, then the stock, in stages so it wouldn't go lumpy.

40 g unsalted butter
¼ cup (35 g) plain flour
1 cup (250 ml) full-cream milk
1 cup (250 ml) Golden Chicken
    Stock (see page 132)
¼ cup (60 ml) verjuice (see page 141)
pinch of grated nutmeg
pinch of ground cinnamon
2 tablespoons grated Parmigiano Reggiano
sea salt and freshly ground white pepper

1 Melt butter in a saucepan over medium heat, then remove from heat and stir in flour. Return pan to stove over low heat, stirring constantly with a wooden spoon for 3–4 minutes or until it turns very light golden (this is just to cook the flour, so it doesn't taste raw). Stirring continuously, pour in milk and mix until incorporated.

2 Gradually stir in stock, adding ¼ cup (60 ml) at a time so the mixture doesn't become lumpy. Increase heat to low–medium and bring to the boil, stirring continuously, then cook for 5 minutes or until sauce starts to thicken (it should bubble gently). Stir in verjuice; the sauce should now be thick enough to coat the back of a spoon. Stir in nutmeg, cinnamon and Parmigiano and season to taste. If not using immediately, cover surface of sauce closely with plastic film to stop a skin forming.

Tomato sugo

Tomato sugo is coarser than tomato passata as it is made from chopped tomatoes, whereas the tomatoes for passata are sieved, making it more like a puree. It can be used in soups, stews and sauces, or any other dish where a tomato flavour is desired, but without the texture or acidity of fresh tomatoes.

20 g unsalted butter
2 tablespoons extra virgin olive oil
1 large onion, finely chopped
2 cloves garlic, finely chopped
⅓ cup (80 ml) red-wine vinegar
1 × 410 g tin chopped Italian tomato
1½ teaspoons caster sugar
1½ teaspoons sea salt
freshly ground black pepper

1 Heat butter and olive oil in a saucepan over low heat, then add onion and garlic and cook, stirring occasionally, for 10 minutes or until caramelised. Increase heat to high, then add vinegar and reduce until evaporated. Add tomato, then return to the boil and cook for 3 minutes. Add sugar and salt and season with pepper, then reduce heat to low and gently simmer for another 15 minutes or until sauce thickens and most of liquid has reduced. Store in and airtight container in the fridge for up to 3 days.

Flo Beer's pickled quince

This is a sentimental dish for me. My late mother-in-law Flo cooked this for me the first time I met the family, and that was the day I fell in love with quinces (it was the first time I'd ever tasted quince). The quince gradually attains a rosy glow as it cooks, but will only develop the deep ruby-red colour over time in the jar. (It will need to mature for several weeks before using.) Cook the quince at just a simmer until soft; don't overcook it in an attempt to colour it as the wedges will lose their shape.

1 kg quinces
juice of ½ lemon
3 cups (750 ml) white-wine vinegar
375 g caster sugar
3 teaspoons cloves
1 tablespoon black peppercorns

1 Wash, peel and core quinces, then cut into quarters or sixths (depending on size), retaining skins and cores. Place cut quinces immediately in a bowl of water with lemon juice added to prevent discolouration.

2 Wrap and tie reserved skins and cores in a piece of muslin. Place vinegar, caster sugar, spices and muslin bag in a large heavy-based saucepan over high heat and cook for 10 minutes or until a thin syrup begins to form. Remove muslin bag, then add quince wedges to the pan and place the muslin bag on top. Simmer over low heat for 20–40 minutes or until the quince starts to turn pink.

3 Remove muslin bag then, using a slotted spoon, transfer quince to clean, dry jars. When each jar is almost full, bring the syrup back to the boil, then transfer to a heatproof jug and pour into each jar to cover the quince. Seal jars, then invert and leave to cool completely. (The colour of the quince will deepen in the jar over time. Leave for several weeks before opening.) Once opened, store in the fridge.

Morello cherry spoon sweets

I use the word 'sweet' in the recipe title, however, this is really sweet-and-sour. Whilst it is wonderful spooned onto thick slices of wholemeal toast with lashings of butter, it's also a great accompaniment for a grilled or barbecued duck breast (see page 59), terrine or even a wedge of cheese.

½ cup (110 g) white sugar
90 g morello cherries, pitted
½ small cinnamon stick
zest of 1 lemon, removed in thin strips with
    a vegetable peeler, leaving the bitter pith
2 teaspoons lemon juice

1 Dissolve sugar in 2 cups (500 ml) water in a saucepan over low heat. Add cherries, cinnamon and lemon zest and simmer for 20 minutes or until syrupy and viscous. Remove from heat.

2 Add lemon juice, then leave to cool. Serve. Store in an airtight container in the fridge for up to 3 days.

Homemade pasta is one of the best things to prepare with a helper in tow.

2⅔ cups (500 g) strong plain flour
1 teaspoon sea salt
4 × 61 g eggs
1–2 egg yolks, as needed

1 Mix flour with salt, then spread on a bench over an area 30 cm in diameter. Make a well in centre, leaving a bank of flour around edge. Break eggs into well, then add 1 egg yolk. Using one hand, combine eggs and yolk until they're amalgamated, and then, using a fork held in the other hand, scoop the flour a little at a time from flour 'banks' into egg mixture, incorporating eggs and flour with your hand. If you feel mixture is too dry, add remaining egg yolk, working it in the same way. Keep doing this until mixture becomes a paste.

2 Scrape up flour and dough, gathering the mass and smearing it across the bench with a pastry scraper until it comes together. Knead dough for 6–10 minutes, pushing it away from you with the heel of your hand, then turning it a quarter to the right, folding dough over, pushing it away and so on. Once dough is shiny and silky, roll it into a ball and wrap it in plastic film. Rest dough in the refrigerator for 30 minutes.

3 Place a pasta machine on a bench, screwing it down firmly. Cut dough into 10 even pieces and cover with a tea towel. Take one piece of dough and press it as flat as you can with the palm of your hand or a rolling pin, then feed it through rollers set on their widest aperture. Fold dough in thirds, then pass narrow end through machine again. Repeat several times, preferably until you hear a sound I can only describe as a 'plop' – this is the tension of the dough releasing as it goes through the rollers.

4 Adjust machine to next setting and pass dough through. Repeat this with every setting until you get to the last, and finest, one. As dough moves through each setting the sheets will become finer and finer; you may need to cut sheets into smaller pieces to make them more manageable. Repeat this process with remaining dough. Proceed as described in the relevant recipe.

Sour-cream pastry

MAKES ENOUGH TO LINE TWO 20–24 CM TART TINS

Always make pastry in the coolest part of the day. The amount of sour cream required here will depend on the flour used and weather conditions. It is difficult to make this pastry in a small quantity, so I recommend making the full amount when you wish to use it, then dividing the pastry in two and wrapping both pieces in plastic film. Chill one piece in the refrigerator for at least 20 minutes, then proceed with the recipe and freeze the second piece to use another time.

1⅔ cups (250 g) plain flour, plus
    extra for dusting
200 g chilled unsalted butter, chopped
½ cup (120 g) sour cream, or more if required

1 Process flour and butter in a food processor until it resembles coarse breadcrumbs. With the motor running, gradually add about two-thirds of the sour cream at first, then add only enough of the remaining sour cream for the pastry to just come together to form a ball (you may need to add a little extra).

2 Turn out pastry onto a lightly floured bench and bring it together into a rectangle with your hands, then wrap in plastic film and chill in the refrigerator for at least 20 minutes. Proceed as described in the relevant recipe.

Gluten-free pastry

MAKES ENOUGH TO LINE TWO 20–24 CM TART TINS

I thought it really important to come up with a gluten-free pastry as more-ish as my sour-cream pastry after being approached by coeliac friends who yearned for the melt-in-the-mouth pastry they'd enjoyed before their diagnosis. I feel this pastry achieves this.

500 g chilled cream cheese, cut into chunks
300 g chilled unsalted butter, chopped
4 cups (600 g) gluten-free flour (see page 141),
    plus extra for dusting
2 tablespoons salt
8 g xanthum gum (available from health-food
    stores and large supermarkets)

1 Pulse cream cheese and butter in a food processor until combined. Add flour, salt and xanthum gum, then whiz to just combine, scraping down the side of the bowl with a spatula. If pastry doesn't come together to form a ball after a few pulses, add a little chilled water (1 tablespoon at the most).

2 Turn dough out onto a bench dusted with a little extra gluten-free flour. Bring dough together with your hands, then knead for 3–4 minutes or until it comes together to form a ball. Although this pastry does not need to be chilled for a long time, it is easier to handle if placed in the refrigerator for 5 minutes before rolling out. (Leftover pastry scraps can be wrapped in plastic film and refrigerated for a few weeks. It can be used to make a quick cheese tart or topped with fruit such as apples, pears or berries for a sweet tart.)

Grilled semolina

2 cups (500 ml) milk
1 fresh bay leaf
1 cup (180 g) instant semolina
1 teaspoon salt
plain flour, for dusting
extra virgin olive oil, for cooking
unsalted butter, for cooking

1 Bring milk, 2 cups (500 ml) water and bay leaf to the boil over high heat in a saucepan, then remove from heat and leave to infuse for 20 minutes. Strain into a heavy-based saucepan, discarding bay leaf, then bring to the boil again. Reduce heat to low. Slowly pour in semolina and add salt, then whisk continuously to combine for 4–5 minutes, ensuring there are no lumpy bits. Grease a baking dish with olive oil, then pour semolina mixture into the dish. Cover with plastic film and leave to set in the refrigerator for at least 2–3 hours.

2 Cut semolina on the diagonal into 7 cm pieces. Lightly dust each piece with flour, then heat a splash of olive oil and a knob of butter in a chargrill pan over high heat and cook semolina pieces for 2 minutes on each side or until warmed through and grill marks appear. Serve.

Creme anglaise

2 cups (500 ml) milk
2 cups (500 ml) double cream
1 vanilla bean, halved lengthways
8 egg yolks
120 g caster sugar
ice cubes

1 Bring milk and cream to the boil in a heavy-based saucepan, then remove from the heat. Scrape in vanilla seeds, then add vanilla bean and leave to infuse. Whisk egg yolks and sugar until thick and pale. Carefully stir heated milk mixture into egg mixture.

2 Return the creme to the pan and heat over low heat, stirring gently and constantly with a wooden spoon until mixture begins to thicken. Take mixture off the heat from time to time if it looks like it is getting too hot. Have a large bowl of iced water standing by in case you take the creme too far and need to place the pan in iced water to cool it down quickly. The custard should be thick enough to coat a wooden spoon and leave a trail when you draw your finger across it. Remove vanilla bean. Serve.

Glossary

Cornichons
These tiny, crisp gherkins are picked when they are 3–8 cm long, and pickled in vinegar or brine.

Gluten-free flour
Ready-made gluten-free flour is available from larger supermarkets and health-food stores, but I like to mix my own. I use equal quantities of potato flour, rice flour and maize flour.

Preserved lemons
These lemons have been preserved in salt (sometimes with the addition of aromatics such as bay leaves, cinnamon, cloves, coriander seeds or peppercorns) and are commonly used in Moroccan cooking. Available in jars from larger supermarkets and select delicatessens.

Ras el hanout
A Moroccan spice blend that includes spices such as paprika, cumin, ginger, coriander seed, cassia, turmeric, fennel seed, allspice, cardamom, nutmeg, caraway seed and cloves. Available from specialty food stores.

Sherry vinegar
A Spanish vinegar made from sherry aged in oak barrels. The best-quality vinegars come from the sherry-producing region of Jerez in Spain. Available from specialty food stores and select delicatessens.

Verjuice
Made from the juice of unfermented grapes, use it as an acidulant wherever you might find lemon juice or vinegar too tart.

Vino cotto
Literally meaning 'cooked wine' in Italian, this traditional Italian preparation is made by simmering unfermented grape juice until it is reduced to a syrup.

Index

LANTERN

Published by the Penguin Group
Penguin Group (Australia)
707 Collins Street, Melbourne, Victoria 3008, Australia
(a division of Penguin Australia Pty Ltd)
Penguin Group (USA) Inc.
375 Hudson Street, New York, New York 10014, USA
Penguin Group (Canada)
90 Eglinton Avenue East, Suite 700, Toronto, Canada ON M4P 2Y3
(a division of Penguin Canada Books Inc.)
Penguin Books Ltd
80 Strand, London WC2R 0RL, England
Penguin Ireland
25 St Stephen's Green, Dublin 2, Ireland
(a division of Penguin Books Ltd)
Penguin Books India Pvt Ltd
11 Community Centre, Panchsheel Park, New Delhi – 110 017, India
Penguin Group (NZ)
67 Apollo Drive, Rosedale, Auckland 0632, New Zealand
(a division of Penguin New Zealand Pty Ltd)
Penguin Books (South Africa) (Pty) Ltd
Rosebank Office Park, Block D, 181 Jan Smuts Avenue,
Parktown North, Johannesburg 2196, South Africa
Penguin (Beijing) Ltd
7F, Tower B, Jiaming Center, 27 East Third Ring Road North,
Chaoyang District, Beijing 100020, China

Penguin Books Ltd, Registered Offices: 80 Strand,
London, WC2R 0RL, England

First published by Penguin Group (Australia), 2012

10 9 8 7 6 5

Text copyright © Maggie Beer 2012

Photographs copyright © Simon Griffiths
(pages 2, 9, 11, 13, 14, 17, 19, 20, 23, 25, 28, 45, 47, 49, 50,
53, 55, 57, 58, 63, 65, 67, 73, 74, 77, 84, 87, 89, 91, 92, 96,
104, 109, 113, 114, 117, 123, 129, 134, 140)

Photographs copyright © Mark Chew
(pages 27, 35, 36, 41, 61, 69, 79, 80, 83, 95, 111, 119, 121, 124)

Photographs copyright © Sharyn Cairns
(pages 31, 33, 39, 71, 99, 103, 106, 127)

Design by Lantern Studio © Penguin Group (Australia)
Typeset in Alright Sans and Adobe Caslon
by Post Pre-press Group, Brisbane, Queensland
Colour reproduction by Splitting Image, Clayton, Victoria
Printed in China by Everbest Printing Co Ltd

National Library of Australia
Cataloguing-in-Publication data:

Beer, Maggie.
Maggie Beer / Maggie Beer

    9781921383144 (pbk.)

    Lantern cookery classics.
    Includes index.

    Cooking.

    641.5

penguin.com.au/lantern